The School Buddy System

The Practice of Collaboration

GAIL BUSH

AMERICAN LIBRARY ASSOCIATION

Chicago
2003

While extensive effort has gone into ensuring the reliability of information appearing in this book, the publisher makes no warranty, express or implied, on the accuracy or reliability of the information, and does not assume and hereby disclaims any liability to any person for any loss or damage caused by errors or omissions in this publication.

Project editor, Eloise L. Kinney

Composition by ALA Editions in Palatino and Flare Gothic using QuarkXPress 4.0 on a PC platform

Printed on 50-pound white offset, a pH-neutral stock, and bound in 10-point cover stock by McNaughton & Gunn

The paper used in this publication meets the minimum requirements of American National Standard for Information Sciences—Permanence of Paper for Printed Library Materials, ANSI Z39.48-1992. ∞

Library of Congress Cataloging-in-Publication Data
Bush, Gail
    The school buddy system : the practice of collaboration / Gail Bush.
        p.   cm.
    Includes bibliographical references and index.
    ISBN 0-8389-0839-X
    1. Teaching teams. 2. Group work in education.   I. Title.
    LB1029.T4 B87 2002
    371.14'8—dc21   2002008315

Printed in the United States of America

07   06   05   04   03   5   4   3   2   1

 *For Rob*

 *Contents*

Preface   *vii*

Acknowledgments   *xiii*

PART I   READY

1 Educator Collaboration Today   1
Definitions of Collaboration   2
Constructing Collaboratively   4
Creating Collaboratively   6

2 Collaboration in Context   9
Two Decades of Reform   *9*
Collaboration Studies   *10*
A Balanced View of Collaboration   *11*
Leadership in Collaborative Models   *15*

3 The Teaching Profession   18
The Culture of Teaching   *19*
Teacher Education   *25*
Societal Influences on Education   *32*

4 Teaching and Learning   37
Thinking   *38*
Social Learning   *40*
Constructivism   *43*

5 The Professional Community   47
New Scholarship   *47*
Teacher/Action/Insider/Practitioner Research   *48*
The "How-To" of Teacher Research   *48*
Communities of Scholar-Teachers   *50*

Professional Development   *52*

Job-Embedded Learning   *53*

From PDS to BRT   *54*

PART II   SET

6 A Collaborative Mind-Set   **57**

Metacognition   *58*

Mindfulness   *59*

Critical Thinking   *62*

Creative Thinking   *64*

Habits of Mind   *66*

Social Justice   *68*

7 Educator Collaboration: A Framework and Reflections   **71**

Why Are We Discussing Collaboration in the Schools?   *72*

Framework of Educator Collaboration   *74*

Framework Reflections   *81*

PART III   DIVE

8 The School Buddy System   **85**

What, Then, Is at Issue?   *86*

Lesson Study (*Jugyou Kenkyuu*)   *88*

Just One Piece of the Puzzle   *91*

The Collaboration Conversation Continues   *91*

The School Buddy System   *93*

9 Conversation Prompts   **95**

Bibliography   *129*

Index   *141*

 *Preface*

The term *collaboration* is used in a variety of ways in education, including school-university, school-parent/community, site-based decision making, and teacher problem solving. Collaborative experiences among educators who have the shared goal of improved student achievement are the driving force of this book. Core elements of collaboration in the schools are identified and explored in an attempt to form a common language. Having read many studies on the topic, it seemed to me there was a void that needed to be filled before we could all start to collaborate on an equal footing.

There is an image that I find useful to illustrate this point. Think about that time in your life when you learned to dive. Standing by the side of the pool, we learned the proper stance: hand over hand, fingers pointed together in a V-shape, head tucked, elbows straight covering our ears, knees bent, and toes curled over the edge of the pool. That is the stance—for better or, in some cases, for worse. The body of literature that is growing concerning collaboration has us already positioned in that stance and ready to dive into the pool. *The School Buddy System* is designed to take us one giant step back from the edge. How do we get into the stance that prepares us for collaboration? How do we become poised to dive in?

Before We Begin

Whenever you start to learn from another person, it is advised that you understand "where they are coming from." I have heard tales of a social science professor at a renowned university who spends the first two lectures of each class talking about his own personal, educational, and professional background; his achievements; and his research interests. Initially it sounds self-serving, but in fact it benefits the students much more than if he dove into the material and taught as if he were an impartial expert in his field. As objective as we attempt to be, we are all human, and each one of us is the sum total of our life experiences. The topics any researcher or author chooses to study and write are direct reflections of matters of importance to her. And that importance is gleaned from what the researcher or author references in her own experiences.

Understanding this stance may help you get through the following sections that delve deeply into the educational research surrounding collaboration in the schools. So what does the educated reader want? An author who is so objective as to deliver the material in a dry and impersonal manner or an author to whom the subject is of personal interest and thereby invests herself in the researching and the writing? Here you have the latter.

I believe very strongly that it is because I came to schools as a professional librarian first that I have been effective in promoting collaborative experiences with educators. I was able to bring a fresh perspective to our library program. As an academic and corporate librarian, my position was one that was respected by my colleagues. Collaboration with colleagues was an essential facet of my responsibilities, especially as a corporate library manager for an international executive recruiting firm. These high-powered associates knew the monetary value of collaborating with an information specialist. Coming into the schools after having a career as a professional librarian was by far the road less traveled.

I returned to graduate school to take the classes needed to enter the public school system. In a school library administration course, I learned that I should keep the coffee hot and conjure up inventive ways to entice teachers to collaborate with me. I was warned about trying to work with teachers. I was confused.

I accepted a position as librarian at a suburban public high school. I observed this new (to me) culture to find clues about the teachers' habits and belief systems. As I read Dan Lortie's *Schoolteacher*, the works of John Goodlad, Seymour Sarason, and others, I began to learn about the culture of teaching. Meanwhile, our library program was recognized as the American Association of School Librarians National School Library Media Program of the Year in 1996. Collaboration features prominently in the recognition of my library partners and our work in the high school library media center.

As our work in the school library field was being recognized, I began working on a doctorate in educational psychology at Loyola University Chicago. I discovered that the body of literature about collaboration was growing exponentially. I conducted a pilot study looking for evidence of instruction in collaboration in teacher education programs.

I found that collaboration was turning up in every new set of standards and guidelines in every area of education. Skills, dimensions, and steps abound. But still, I had not found (and others who have been researching collaboration concur) a place to begin. A place where we step back from the edge and say, Let's think about these things and then we will start to figure this out together. Can collaboration be taught? Administrators say, in hushed voices, maybe it IS personality. What then?

I say, I don't think so. That is too simple, too dismissive. As a librarian I have heard more than my share about personality over the years.

There are elements that we can identify and support. We can build a knowledge base that sits on a foundation of collaboration that is set out in this framework. We can use a common language that will facilitate our work and our discussions. Scholars in areas of specialization within education can take this structure and build their own models to satisfy the needs of their practitioners. I invite my colleagues in education to use this book and the *Framework of Educator Collaboration* in chapter 7 as a basis for further study. I encourage you to adapt it to your needs. Along with my fellow librarians, I do not believe in the value of knowledge that is not shared. I plan to continue this work, and I hope that my efforts will benefit others in their pursuits.

Piscem Natare Doces

You are teaching a fish to swim. Why write a book about something as obvious as collaboration? What will we learn from this research that we don't already know?

Piscem natare doces. According to some critics of social research, this Latin expression could be applied to many of the findings of qualitative research studies. Gage (1993) explores this view in his chapter, "The Obviousness of Social and Educational Research Results," in Hammersley's *Social Research: Philosophy, Politics and Practice.* He traces this charge back to the late 1940s, when sociologists were studying the attitudes of American soldiers during World War II. Gage quotes sociologist Lazarsfeld's conclusions: "Obviously something is wrong with the entire argument of obviousness. It should really be turned on its head. Since every kind of human reaction is conceivable, it is of great importance to know which reactions actually occur most frequently and under what conditions" (p. 234).

In the field of education, Gage reports that the studies of fourth- and sixth-graders by Mischel and Mischel in the 1970s and Baratz's 1983 study of college students contain persuasive evidence that could be used against the argument that social research in education yields only obvious findings. Consider Gage's examination of relevant studies and argument that even when social research findings do concur with common beliefs, they shed light on when and how the "truism" applies to particular cases. These are concerns that continue to plague social research. Keeping Gage's viewpoint in mind, we turn to Pintrich's (1994) conclusion to his article, "Continuities and Discontinuities: Future Directions for Research in Educational Psychology." Pintrich reminds us that "the importance of psychological perspectives and our passionate intensity for improving education" (p. 148) are what hold us together as educational psychologists. I find that both Gage and Pintrich speak to the topic of this book.

There are those critics who might declare that the subject of this study is "obvious." In fact, different participants commented on contradicting points as being self-evident. Yet it is that passionate intensity for improving education that drives me to dig deeply into the phenomenon of collaboration, to study this educational hot topic, and to stake out that fertile ground that makes collaborative experiences bloom. What elements are present and what do we call them? How do we start to communicate among ourselves, educator to educator, to begin the process of goal-oriented collaboration in the schools? Effective action research teams are discovering strategies and tools within the realm of professional development (Cochran-Smith & Lytle, 1993; Burnaford et al., 1996; Duckworth, 1997; Lambert et al., 1997). Our mutual goal is to ensure that all of our efforts reach future teachers, school librarians, and students and do not end up sitting on the shelf with the other staff development packages that delivered last year's hot topic in education.

The Information Revolution

Are we still revolving? It is time to stop spinning and begin to understand the significant impact on the manner in which we do business in schools. Of course, many of the studies and sources mentioned in this book were conducted and published before the information revolution was upon us. More to the point. They do not even take into consideration the changes that have befallen education. The multimedia educational technology, the availability of vast quantities of information, the availability of e-mail for students, and the omnipresence of the Internet all have impacted the isolation of the classroom. No longer can a teacher completely control the availability of resources and information flowing to her students.

Information has always been the domain of the library, stored and retrieved by librarians for centuries dating back to Alexandria. That has not changed with the information revolution. Librarians have been using computers and have been retrieving information online using telephone lines since the mid-1970s. The prototypes of computer-assisted instruction were developed at the Computer-Based Education Research Laboratory at the University of Illinois Urbana-Champaign campus in the early 1970s. Computer technology has been a required course in the training of librarians since that time (library automation and computer programming courses). The latest edition of *Information Power: Building Partnerships for Learning (IP2)* was published in partnership by the

American Association of School Librarians (a division of the American Library Association) and the Association for Educational Communications and Technology (1998b). *IP2* has a focus on collaboration and leadership beyond the information revolution.

The varied roles of the school librarian include information specialist, instructional consultant, teacher, and educational leader. None of these roles can be successful in schools without effective collaboration with classroom teachers, administrators, other professionals, the community, and even resource persons available online. The "learning community" as defined by *IP2* is a "global web of individuals and organizations that are interconnected in a lifelong quest to understand and meet constantly changing information needs" (p. 122).

The school learning community is an all-inclusive concept that enfolds all adults in the school environment who impact students. Support staff are often overlooked, as are administrators and community members. We all have a stake in our students' success. Coming together as goal-oriented collaborators not only provides a richer, more textured learning environment for our students, we also model an important facet of living and working together in this modern age of information and communication. The fears that many have about telecommunications having an isolating effect on our youth can be counter-balanced by providing role models who come together with purpose and create outcomes that inform and inspire young minds.

My lens is multifaceted. The combination of anthropology and educational psychology places my cultural studies firmly in the school learning community. My research laboratory is nestled in the library, which can be seen as both marginal in the school setting to those in the classroom and focal in the sense of being the hub of the school learning environment. Your academic and/or experiential background will determine what you will glean from this work, what you will put to use, store for later, discard from the get-go. It is your responsibility to apply what is applicable, to look at something or someone in a new light, to relate these chapters to your own personal situation in your school or class. This book is my offering; the rest is up to you. Let's hope that together we can make this a worthwhile endeavor that will ultimately benefit all of our learners.

 *Acknowledgments*

There is a Buddhist saying that when the student is ready, a teacher will appear.

I have had many teachers along this journey. Everything I learned about collaboration during my career as a librarian was because of the generosity of the many people with whom I worked. Most recently, the administration, faculty, students, and staff at Maine West High School in Des Plaines, Illinois, especially Merrilee Andersen Kwielford, Geralyn Haan, Sally Tibbetts, Anna Volas, and Georgia Knoblock, have given of themselves so freely and have continued to support my professional endeavors.

The value of this book would not be as substantial without the thoughtful responses from the practitioners and education scholars who gave of their valuable time to contribute their unique views on the subject. Excerpts from their comments can be found sprinkled throughout the text to add flavor and insight from yet another perspective.

I am indebted to each and every one of them:

Gail C. Bailey, Branch Chief
    School Library Media Services and State Media Services Branch
    Maryland State Department of Education
    Baltimore, Maryland

Camille L. Z. Blachowicz, Director
    National Reading Center
    National-Louis University
    Evanston, Illinois

Carolyn Bohlman, ESL/BE Teacher
    Maine East High School
    Des Plaines, Illinois

Betty A. Brockelman, Assistant Superintendent
    Curriculum and Instruction
    New Trier High School
    Winnetka, Illinois

Edward L. Chartraw, Retired Superintendent of Schools
  Country Club Hills School District 160
  Country Club Hills, Illinois

Michelle Commeryas, Associate Professor
  Reading and Teacher Education
  University of Georgia
  Athens, Georgia

Sharon Cramer, Chairperson
  Exceptional Education Graduate Program
  Buffalo State College, SUNY
  Buffalo, New York

Celeste DiCarlo-Nalwasky, Director
  Information Services
  Intermediate Unit I
  Regional Educational Service Agency
  Coal Center, Pennsylvania

Emerson J. Elliott, Director
  Program Standards Development Project
  National Council for Accreditation of Teacher Education (NCATE)
  Washington, D.C.

Declan T. FitzPatrick, Language Arts Teacher
  Ladue Horton Watkins High School
  St. Louis, Missouri

Violet H. Harada, Associate Professor
  School of Library and Information Science
  University of Hawaii
  Honolulu, Hawaii

G. Alfred Hess Jr., Professor of Learning Sciences
  Northwestern University
  Evanston, Illinois

Lynn Hiller, Special Education Department Coordinator
  New Trier High School
  Winnetka, Illinois

Lynn McCarthy, Assistant Superintendent
Building Operations
Evanston Elementary School District 65
Evanston, Illinois

Gillian McNamee, Director
Teacher Education and Child Development
Erikson Institute
Chicago, Illinois

Danette Erickson Meyer, ESL/BE Consultant and Teacher
Illinois Resource Center
Des Plaines, Illinois

Jeremy Perney, Former Language Arts Teacher
Maine West High School
Des Plaines, Illinois

Robin J. Perrone, Reading Specialist and Language Arts Teacher
Maine West High School
Des Plaines, Illinois

Lynne M. Schrum, Associate Professor
Department of Instructional Technology
University of Georgia
Athens, Georgia

Dennis Sparks, Executive Director
National Staff Development Council (NSDC)
Ann Arbor, Michigan

Lucy Steiner, Educational Researcher and Consultant
Public Impact
Chapel Hill, North Carolina

Ann Carlson Weeks, Former Director
Libraries and Information Services
Chicago Public Schools
Chicago, Illinois

Marshall Welch, Department Chair
Special Education, Graduate School of Education
University of Utah
Salt Lake City, Utah

Denise Winter, Principal
Stone Scholastic Academy
Chicago, Illinois

I enjoyed unwavering support from mentors, especially Ronald R. Morgan at Loyola University Chicago and Ann D. Carlson at Dominican University, friends, and family. Many thanks to my editing buddy, Eloise L. Kinney, and to Patrick Hogan and the staff at ALA Editions for their patience, insight, and good work. Finally, to Rob and Matt and Claire, a heartfelt thank-you for believing in me and in our family.

CHAPTER **1**

Educator Collaboration Today

There is no doubt about it. *Collaboration* is a buzzword. It's hot. You can find reference to it in virtually every field from nonprofits to business, from education to medicine. Grant funds are flowing to projects that promise collaboration among colleagues. The popularity of the term itself causes serious students in any of these fields to question the gravitas of the subject. The very timeliness of a hot topic taints it as ephemeral. Why learn about something that is in today but will be tomorrow's old news?

While the term *collaboration* is one that appears to be current, the topic has been around in various forms throughout the ages. Today we view it as a fresh idea grown out of the work of those who have come before. Famous collaborative teams have given us inventions and discoveries, from airplanes to DNA, that improve the quality of our daily lives.

Sometimes collaboration is not obvious at first glance. The assumption that this book is an individual study conducted by the author alone is subject to question. Any researcher knows that when we apply the work of others to our ideas and give birth to something new, we owe much to the great thinkers who paved the way ahead of us. In truth, this work is a collaborative effort substantiated by some of the great minds of all time, starting with Socrates.

Let's begin by pondering what it was about Socrates that led his contemporaries and those who followed to believe that he changed, even revolutionized, the pattern of thought. Philosophers tell us that it was not the deep profundity of his revelations but rather the simplicity, "principles almost too obvious to need expression, and almost too general to be capable of expression . . . like the air we breathe, such a form (of thought) is so translucent, and so pervading, and so seemingly necessary, that only by extreme effort can we become aware of it" (Whitehead in Sinaiko, 1998, p. 7).

It was the focus that Socrates gave to talk, discourse, the communication between two persons that is so startlingly basic. In Socrates' view, that discourse is actually a search for truth and therefore a search for self-knowledge (Sinaiko, 1998). To Socrates it is not the image of Rodin's lone thinker with head in hand that will gain true knowledge but it is a communal experience, conversational and dialogical. Those with whom Socrates dialogued were necessary to Socrates himself because of the communal nature of his philosophy. His respect for his students was genuine because he believed that we are all equals in the search for self-knowledge. And still, he demanded much from those students. They needed to have disciplined minds that could follow arguments and actively participate in the ambitious and protracted Socratic quest for truth. The prolific scholar and educator Howard Gardner shares this belief and toward this goal recommends the exploration of truth, beauty, and goodness as a method of enhancing students' deep understanding (1999a).

> **Cultural Perspectives**
>
> Is collaboration a concept that would be defined similarly across cultures? Individualism is a very Western concept. Collaboration in other societies is the norm—the way everything is done.
> —*Teacher Educator*

DEFINITIONS OF COLLABORATION

Collaboration is goal-oriented talk, discourse, conversation, communication, in this case, between two or more educators. It is a way for educators to search for self-knowledge as professionals by engaging in dialogue with colleagues who share a goal for their students. It is in the process of this search that we come to know ourselves as teachers in a way that is not possible when the classroom door is shut tight and the journey toward wisdom is not shared. This sounds contradictory—both to seek self-knowledge and to share that journey. It is in the sharing that we gain knowledge about ourselves that would not be possible without listening to a different perspective, point of view, angle, vantage point. The act of sharing our thoughts with others forces us to express and thereby acknowledge those thoughts to ourselves. We are, after all, only human. We cannot see everything from all sides. That is why, as we all dwell in the human condition, we need the companionship of our colleagues, who can share in the journey and add texture to our solitary view of the world. Anthropologist Edward T. Hall (1976) contends that there is a natural drive to collaborate. He considers this drive to be one of the basic principles of living.

Like everything else in life, some of us come by this stance naturally. There are teachers who are "naturals" and there are others who work hard to make it their own. Because of the naturals, there are those who think that the elements necessary for collaboration cannot be taught to

the rest of us. Imagine, with such a preponderance of interest in collaboration, that we are merely relying on our personality and interpersonal skills to carry the day. If that were the case, we would not need teacher education programs. After all, if we were all naturals, why teach anyone how to be a teacher? Or how to be a leader? We need to give every educator the same chance at success just like we all agree that we need to give every student an equal chance to learn. Sometimes those who are explicitly taught become dedicated educators who work very hard and impact student learning in a way that the rest of us cannot touch. Those dedicated educators may be thirty-year veterans or new teachers fresh out of preparatory programs. It is folly to think that we can classify who is a better teacher by the number of years of experience. We should not count out any of our colleagues on the basis of age and/or tenure. The teaching cycle can work for or against an educator's ability to see her students and colleagues with fresh eyes.

In *The Culture of Education* educational anthropologist Jerome S. Bruner (1996) defines collaboration as "sharing the resources of the mix of human beings involved in teaching and learning" (p. 87). This definition speaks to the collaborative mix of educators

A
Common Ground

Community presupposes a knowledge about and familiarity with others in your department, building, and district—a common ground and bond which allows for comfortable sharing.
—Administrator

from different professional cultural biases working together in the schools. Writing "In Honor of Anselm Strauss: Collaboration," Barney G. Glaser (1995) "never realized that people could truly collaborate. Collaboration so often fails in a cloud of mutual distrust and hatred. It can be a treacherous and dangerous business" (p. 103). Collaboration can mean many different things to educators depending on their perceptions of their students' needs (Sarason, 1971).

Not all talk is collaboration, and collaboration in the schools takes more than just talk between two or more educators. Russian psychologist Lev Vygotsky (1962) connects learners (read educators) as active organizers who need social interchange in order to become aware of and understand what is going on around us and to then use language to change both the world and ourselves. Collaboration in the most effective situations includes a shared vision (Senge et al., 1994) and a whole that is greater than the sum of the parts. In his book *Shared Minds: The New Technologies of Collaboration* Michael Schrage (1990) defines collaboration as "the process of shared creation—two or more individuals with complementary skills interacting to create a shared understanding that none had previously possessed or could have come to on their own" (p. 40).

Vera John-Steiner (1997) writes about Olby's account of Crick and Watson and their discovery of DNA. Olby, a science historian, quotes Alexander Humboldt to describe Crick and Watson's collaboration: "Collaboration operates through a process in which the successful intellectual achievements of one person arouse the intellectual passions and enthusiasms of others, and through the fact that what was at first expressed only by one individual becomes a common intellectual possession instead of fading away into isolation" (pp. 187-188). Another scientific collaborative partnership, of Bohr and Heisenberg, led to the understanding of quantum physics. In the arts, we have the collaborative pairings of Braque and Picasso, Gilbert and Sullivan, and Rogers and Hammerstein. In business there are many entrepreneurial partnerships, including the Wright brothers and more recently Apple computer founders Jobs and Wozniak. And in mathematics, Einstein had a long collaborative friendship with mathematician Marcel Grossman.

There does seem to be agreement that collaboration, in all its variations, is a dynamic process. There is a collaborative ethic defined by Friend and Cook (2000) as a set of values or principles that endorse collegial versus independent action. They point out the societal perspective that comes from the futurists (e.g., Toffler, 1970). The notion of rugged individualism was important when the United States was settled. However, this individualism included reliance on others such as barn raisings and clearing fields. Now that society is so complex, the time has come again in this information age where reliance on others is key to accomplishing our goals. That collaborative ethic as described by Friend and Cook (2000) where professionals voluntarily work together covers the basic expression of collaboration as a decision-making or problem-solving technique. However, it does not quite go the distance that is reached in this approach where the collaborative process goes beyond that of technique to a state of mind or, more specifically, a collaborative mind-set.

CONSTRUCTING COLLABORATIVELY

A major theme in the contemporary educational theory of constructivism is that learning is an active process in which learners construct new ideas or concepts based on their prior knowledge (Brooks & Brooks, 1993). In this view, knowledge is a constructed entity made by each learner through a learning process. In the context of this book, the teachers are viewed as constructivist learners who are constructing knowledge as they interact with a group of learners. The constructivists see traditional education "as stifling students' creativity, autonomy, independent thinking, competence, confidence, and self-esteem and as making

students dependent, conforming, and nonthinking" (Marlowe & Page, 1998, p. 13). All of this can be said for the teacher who is transmitting the information as well. It is understandable that the view of teachers as learners and social constructors of knowledge is reported to be one of the biggest obstacles for teachers when they make transitions from a teacher-centered to a student-centered theory of teaching and learning (Steffe & Gale, 1995).

It stands to reason that a teacher who expects his or her students to be active, social, creative learners will have a disconnect unless there is an understanding of what that means firsthand. Teachers whose students discuss, debate, and hypothesize, and who create or re-create knowledge in a group setting, must re-evaluate themselves as learners to completely engage in the constructivist educational milieu (Perkins, 1999). This is not to say that the constructivism is an all-or-nothing proposition. Even to merely use this approach where it might logically work better than traditional methods, the teacher is at a disadvantage if she cannot relate to the students as a constructivist learner.

When asked if "this way of teaching" gave her students deeper insights into the texts, teacher Jane Tomkins questions the question: "The question assumes that 'we,' the readers, will somehow be better off if we have 'insight' into 'them,' the texts. For my class, this relation was topsy-turvy. The texts became the scaffolding for the building we were constructing. They were the road we walked on to wherever we were going, the road that allowed us to see" (1996, p. 177). Naturally, this is easier said than done when we consider the uphill battle it is to recognize the traditional educational background of these teachers both as students and in their preservice preparatory programs.

Even teachers who support collaborative learning among their students often have questions about its relevance to the content of the course and whether there is a place for it in their own toolkit of useful skills. It is the self-reflective quest for self-knowledge that endorses collaboration as a valuable asset in one's arsenal. To awaken genius in our students, Thomas Armstrong (1998) advises us to reawaken the genius in ourselves, not so much as educators but as human beings. He cautions us against neglect of our own inner resources of joy, humor, creativity, and wonder. Jersild (1955) wrote over forty-five years ago that teachers need to look within in order to face the task of teaching. More recently, William Ayers (1993) writes in *To Teach: The Journey of a Teacher* that "greatness in teaching requires a serious encounter with autobiography: Who are you? How did you come to take on your views and outlooks? . . . An encounter with these kinds of questions is critical to outstanding teaching because teachers, whatever

> **Become Leaders**
>
> "Teachers who consider themselves to be leaders seek out collaborative experiences." Is it possible that teachers who seek out collaborative experiences become leaders?
>
> *—Policymaker*

 5

else they teach, teach themselves. Of all the knowledge teachers need to draw on, self-knowledge is most important and least attended to" (p. 129).

The Holmes Group, a consortium of research-oriented schools and colleges of education, continued to study concerns in teacher education throughout the 1980s and 1990s. The Holmes Group is now the Holmes Partnership. The publications that came from this coalition led teacher educators to seriously consider collaboration as an essential cog in the re-form machine (Holmes Group, 1986; 1990; 1995). In *Tomorrow's Schools: A Report of the Holmes Group* (1990), collaboration is one of five elements in a core knowledge of all educators. The coalition's latest study has col-laboration running through each chapter, e.g., "From 'My Work' to 'Our Work'" (Holmes Partnership, 1998). Collaboration between universities and schools and action research go hand in hand according to the find-ings related to this latest study.

To actualize and sustain such a collaborative partnership requires a shift in the professional orientation in the preparation of new teachers. This shift raises concerns about who controls knowledge production in education, teachers' voices in guiding professional education programs, and the degree to which change can occur through consensus. Along with these concerns, the shift in professional orientation also renders a new guard of teachers who are more activist in their thinking, who believe that social justice and equity can be striven for through social change, and who feel that they have the power and the responsibility to see that changes in the schools reflect their viewpoint. This new guard paints a very different picture from the practitioner who feels oppressed by standards and the pressure to teach to the standardized test. Someplace in this field there is room to guide teachers of all viewpoints through the collaborative process. In this place, this new comfort zone created as a by-product of the collaborative process, practitioners can work together to provide the best academic experience for their students that their profession has to offer.

CREATING COLLABORATIVELY

Perhaps the professional artistry that Schön (1987) describes in *Educating the Reflective Practitioner* provides a common ground for educators to come together. Like Max DePree's (1992) theme in *Leadership Jazz*, Schön relates the collaboration of musicians to conversation. The pace and rhythm of interaction that may lead to unexpected directions all eventu-ally lead to the making of something. Schön considers conversation to be a product of reflection-in-action. He points to professional artists as those who are skillful improvisers and who create something through this process of conversing. Practitioners in the same profession may dif-fer greatly, and certainly that is true in education. These differences often provide the wealth of riches from which the most effective collaborative experiences come. Collaboration, then, not only provides a common ground but the collaborative process invites divergent thinking and multiple perspectives in order to produce innovative and unique outcomes.

Conversing as artisans in the field of education implies not just talking but listening as well. It is when we actively listen to each other that transformation of thought occurs. In a self-interested way, listening to a colleague provides an opportunity for us to see a different perspective. It is that new viewpoint that brings into focus our own experiences.

A master teacher I worked with bemoans the lack of attention to creativity in schools today. She believes that we educate the creativity out of the students. Can the same be said for teachers? With the strict adherence to the coverage of content within their curricula, teachers have little room for original thought except where it stays within the confines of the prescribed unit. The start-up energy that it takes to begin the collaborative process is more than some teachers are willing to invest. There are circumstances when they believe that their efforts are necessitated not by the curriculum but by other requirements, like a technological tool that modernizes their lessons.

This attention to technology swings both ways. There are teachers who merely tack on a technology component to their pre-existing lesson plans without making it integral to specific learning goals, and there are those who collaborate with others to ensure that the technology component is enhancing the learning experience. Again, one cannot point to the age or tenure of a teacher to predict a predilection for one path or the other. The experienced teacher might be more flexible because of comfort with the content area whereas a younger, more technologically adept teacher might prefer the comfort zone of the classroom because of insecurity in the content area and use technology as a classroom management tool. Trying to predict creativity hardly seems feasible.

Creativity is such an individual human expression, it comes from deep down within ourselves, not from "think[ing] something up" (Cameron, 1992, p. 117). It is a self-reflective process (John-Steiner, 1997; 2000). The demands that educational technology places on the school librarian can actually have a positive impact on her creative thinking abilities (Bush, 2001; Bush & Kwielford, 2001). Psychologist Howard Gruber (in Schrage, 1990) believes that creative people use their skills to create environments that foster their work. "They invent peer groups appropriate to their projects. Each creator therefore invents new forms of collaboration" (p. 44).

It is when we converse and truly listen to our colleagues that we learn about ourselves in the Socratic sense and, in turn, find new ways to share this knowledge. It seems unlikely that teachers who do not experience these acts of reflecting, conversing, and creating community

as described by Schön can guide students to engage in their own thought-provoking conversations.

Writing in "My Pedagogic Creed," John Dewey (1897/1972) stated that he believed that "education must be conceived as a continuing reconstruction of experience; that the process and the goal of education are one and the same thing" (p. 95). Collaboration between educators in the school ensures that they, too, are continuing to reconstruct their experiences and are working together as professionals toward an education where the process and the goal are the same. I hope that reading and discussing the content of this book will make the conversation about collaboration in the schools a little deeper, a little more commonplace, and a little more inclusive.

In the following chapters we consider the frame of reference we have for the study of collaboration within the field of education. We need to be equipped with the big picture of the culture of teaching, teacher education, and societal influences on education. *Education is a research-based applied science.* Throughout, the following features provide guidelines for specific application and concept integration:

> PART I: **Educational research chapters** will give us the foundation we need for a comprehensive grounding in the subject. The many references will lead the inquisitive reader to more in-depth research on each documented study. The collaborative mind-set establishes those characteristics of thought that suggest patterns and practices.

> PART II: A *Framework of Educator Collaboration* is presented to give the readers a structure from which to progress on their journeys, coupled with an invitation to dive into the bottom of the deep. Reflections on the framework illuminate and enhance it for us.

> PART III: **Conversation Prompts** may be used any which way— while reading the book, as weekly exercises throughout the school year, or as a culminating activity after finishing the book the first time around. Throughout this book, there are thought-provoking comments written by experts in the field, including classroom teachers; administrators; professors of teacher education, special education, and library science; and policymakers. These comments cause us to relate what we are reading to a personal reflection, and we, in turn, might choose to discuss, write in a journal, or simply ponder the point as we continue reading.

So now let us relax our stance and take one giant step back from the edge of the pool. Together we will begin to discover what it will take for all of us to be poised to dive into collaboration.

2

Collaboration in Context

TWO DECADES OF REFORM

Trends in the recent history of collaboration studies form the basis for today's "ready to dive" position. Current studies in collaboration within the school follow the educational reforms of the 1980s, when the concept of site-based management (SBM) of schools came into vogue. Where the principal had been operating under the direct aegis of the district, under SBM the principle of self-management prevailed (Pugach & Johnson, 2002). Those who are on-site at the school could best administer to its needs. The main players in this new philosophy of management were the principal (and other administrators), teachers, specialist teachers, support staff, and parents. This decentralization of authority led to team management with representatives of each group of stakeholders making decisions that carried authority within the school. This collegial style of management shared the ownership of the educational program and made everyone a stakeholder in the process. Practices such as mutual help, exchange of ideas, joint planning, and participation in decisions defined a collaborative work setting in both effective schools and successful businesses (Smith & Scott, 1990). These studies which grew out of the SBM reforms of the 1980s focus on the collaboration between teachers and their principals for management purposes and among teachers for problem-solving purposes.

The increased responsibilities of classroom teachers under SBM increased their stature as professionals. Collaborative school environments started the job of opening the classroom door and making teachers mutually responsible for the quality of practice within their schools. The extent to which teachers collaborate with each other within that environment is related to their personalities and prior relationships with colleagues. The collaborative problem-solving models that were developed in the late 1980s and early 1990s depended on two features for a healthy collaborative structure: "(1) the ability to work with others whose professional orientation, talents, and knowledge differ; and (2) the ability to take maximum advantage of the different professional orientations, talents, and knowledge of the individuals in the group" (Hart, 1998, p. 109).

As the changes in management influenced team building in schools in the 1980s, a collaborative process that involved school psychologists, teachers, and parents began to decrease referrals to special education. This consultation-based approach changed the role of the special educator. The new process succeeded where teachers and service providers worked effectively together. The switch from consultation to collaboration came when the role of the special educator "evolved" from that of expert to one of joint problem solver (Cramer, 1998, p. 16). Hudson and Glomb (1997) find that while both special education and general education preparation programs provide preservice teachers with the technical expertise for their respective areas of certification, few programs provide both majors with instruction in interpersonal communication skills and collaboration strategies.

> **Driving the Boat**
>
> Someone has to be driving the boat. Empowerment is essential. People work hard and engage their creativity when they believe that the work they do produces a commensurate outcome that is valued by some community. Teachers who drive collaboration believe that how they teach impacts how students learn.–*Practitioner*

O'Shea and O'Shea (1997) make predictions that link school reform (regarding special education primarily) and collaboration in their article "Collaboration and School Reform: A Twenty-First-Century Perspective." Their ten predictions are based on the importance of strategic planning, shared decision making, and teaming and collaboration. Effective collaboration processes reflect a need to understand multiple perspectives on issues, the ability to compromise, trust others' motivations, and have patience. O'Shea and O'Shea counsel that "students, families, and professionals need to maintain their faith in others and keep their interest from waning on key issues" (p. 460).

COLLABORATION STUDIES

Much of the discussion about collaboration in education centers on teacher-researcher collaborations (Welch, 1998) and the professional development schools (PDSs) movement (Hobbs et al., 1998). The nature of collaboration and collaborative relationships in professional development is explored by Clark, Moss, and Goering (1996) using a Readers Theater script based on meeting dialogues and interaction. John-Steiner,

Weber, and Minnis (1998) respond by suggesting that Clark et al. construct an integrative theory. John-Steiner et al. contend that by looking for commonalities and differences across settings, tasks, working methods, goals, and values, a framework for understanding collaboration can be constructed that preserves the benefits of rich descriptive accounts. Patrick (1999) discusses the social context of teacher preparation at the national and state levels (focusing on Texas) and suggests that a collaborative PDS model of teacher preparation provides the process through which diversity issues are addressed in field-based classrooms. Effective teacher preparation then requires a paradigm shift toward a seamless web of experiences taken from the best practices of schools, universities, communities, and industries.

Several books promoting the collaborative learning environment were published in the middle to late 1990s: *Collaborative Practitioners, Collaborative Schools,* by Pugach and Johnson (2002; second edition); *Interactions: Collaboration Skills for School Professionals,* by Friend and Cook (2000; third edition); *Collaboration: A Success Strategy for Special Educators,* by Cramer (1998); *Restructuring Schools for Collaboration: Promises and Pitfalls,* by Pounder (1998); and *Best Practice: New Standards for Teaching and Learning in America's Schools,* by Zemelman, Daniels, and Hyde (1998; second edition). Each of these books extols the virtues of collaboration and warns the reader of the obstacles to effective collaboration. In these texts, collaboration is viewed in relation to problem solving and teaming and as a product of effective communication. Collaboration is enthusiastically praised as an integral part of constructivism, social learning, professional development, and school reform. Strong recommendations are made to include collaboration in teacher education programs through both course work and university-school partnerships. The challenge to educator collaboration is seen in the barriers presented by the existing structures of a modernistic school system and traditional teaching methods.

A BALANCED VIEW OF COLLABORATION

It is probably fair to say that collaboration is viewed through rose-colored glasses in most accounts. To gain a more balanced picture of collaboration in schools we turn to Rosenholtz (1989), Little (1990), Hargreaves (1994), John-Steiner et al. (1998), and Leonard and Leonard (1999).

Rosenholtz (1989) argues that "when collaborative norms undergird achievement-oriented groups, they bring new ideas, fresh ways of looking at things, and a stock of collective knowledge that is more fruitful

than any one person's working alone" (p. 41). She examines the constraints on collaboration and the way in which teachers go about structuring their collegial relationships. Rosenholtz argues that the norms of self-reliance and teacher uncertainty both function as "double-edged swords" (p. 69). Self-reliance blinds teachers to their colleagues' common problems, serves to make them protective of their own situations, and leads to territoriality. Teacher uncertainty constructs lead teachers to feel shameful of their own inadequacies when they imagine that they alone suffer from instructional problems. Helping behaviors can be very tricky for teachers. Offers to work with colleagues to face instructional challenges threaten a teacher's professional standing by implying that the "donor of the advice is more competent than the recipient" (p. 42). Rosenholtz does not see isolated teachers as lonely so much as suffering from incompleteness.

Teacher leaders who do exist in isolated schools engage in noninstructional activities that remain unthreatening to isolated teachers and administrators. They do not assist in resolving instructional problems. Rosenholtz acknowledges the uncertain principal's role in the inability to facilitate teachers collaborating with one another. Principals who are "more certain" (p. 69) galvanize their faculties in specific goal-directed endeavors and increase their teachers' clarity of purpose. The opportunities principals create for teacher collaboration and their ability to share authority by empowering faculties to make decisions help teachers have a shared sense of school purpose. It is that feeling of responsibility for the school and not just the classroom that is a significant bridge to cross for teachers who profess a commitment to effective collaboration in their schools.

Teacher Leaders

Teachers who are successful leaders are those who seek out collaborative experiences. Some teachers see themselves as leaders, but they are not successful because they are not collaborative.—*Administrator*

Little (1990) argues that teachers are now being "pressed, invited, and cajoled into ventures in 'collaboration,' but the organization of their daily work often gives them scant reason for doing so" (p. 530). Little points to the unwelcome exposure brought by collaboration to the teachers' independent existence within the safe and protective classroom walls. The various forms of teacher exchange that may pass as collegiality may not effect the desired results predicted by the education pundits extolling the wonders of collaboration. Little suggests that those very social interactions that are collaborative in nature may work toward reinforcing the status quo in a school's culture by resisting innovations producing a power-in-numbers scenario.

In *Changing Teachers, Changing Times,* Hargreaves (1994) defines

Organizational Change Strategy

How would a different way of training potential teachers lead to different ways of working in schools when the fundamental culture of schooling mitigates against such an approach? How would training people to work differently from the existing cultural mores of an organization make an effective organizational change strategy?—*Teacher Educator*

contrived collegiality as "teachers' collaborative working relationships (that) are not spontaneous, voluntary, development-oriented, pervasive across time and space and unpredictable" (p. 195). In contrast to collaborative cultures, contrived collegiality is administratively regulated, compulsory, implementation-oriented, fixed in time and space, and predictable. The manifestations of contrived collegiality in Hargreaves's study were mandated collaboration and joint planning in preparation time, required consultation with special education resource teachers at scheduled times, and participation in peer coaching programs. Hargreaves found that two of the major consequences of contrived collegiality were inflexibility and inefficiency as evidenced by teachers not meeting when they should, meeting when there was no business to discuss, and being involved in peer coaching schemes that were misunderstood or where partners were mismatched.

Let's take preparation time as one example of a common starting point for teacher collaboration. Teachers' work is so highly contextualized that Hargreaves sees little value in calculating how many teachers would benefit from minor restructuring such as shared preparation time and how many would not. Presumably, administrators would then decide, based on the numbers, whether to mandate preparation time use. Many teachers benefit from the solitude that preparation time affords them. The capacity to be alone and mentally prepare for the next task is a quality of intellectual maturity. Solitude can stimulate creativity and imagination, which in turn spurs further work. Hargreaves found that aside from preparation time, many teachers point to their cars and their homes as providing a time and place free from distractions. Some teachers see using "my time" (p. 181) for anything like conversation or even relaxation as wasted time. Hargreaves sees the results of mandated collegiality as overriding teachers' professionalism, diverting teachers' energies and efforts. He contends that the salient issue underlying contrived collegiality is one "of willingness to give to schools and their teachers substantial responsibility for development as well as implementation, for curriculum as well as instruction. . . . What remains to be seen, amidst all the rhetoric of restructuring and reform, is whether principals, school system administrators and politicians are prepared to bite that particular bullet" (p. 209).

Contrived collegiality is one of the forms of collaboration that Fullan and Hargreaves (1996; revised edition) recommend we watch carefully. The other two forms are balkanization and comfortable collaboration.

 **13**

In those schools where teachers feel more of an alliance to other teachers than they do in a school culture of isolation, there may be a "balkanized" teacher culture. Fullan and Hargreaves define this as a "culture made up of separate and sometimes competing groups, jockeying for position and supremacy like loosely connected, independent city states" (p. 52). The teachers have loyalty to and identity with particular groups of their colleagues. Balkanization is familiar in high schools where the subject department compartmentalizes the faculty. Even collaborative groups of teachers working diligently on initiatives can affect a singular posture that chooses those aspects of innovations that relate to them; they disregard the rest and other groups that might be constructing initiatives supporting those innovations.

> ## Four Specific Behaviors
>
> Collaboration involves four specific behaviors: educators (1) talk about practice; (2) observe each other; (3) work on curriculum; and (4) teach each other. Knowledge is revealed, articulated, and shared.—*Administrator*

Fullan and Hargreaves also view the group-imposed boundaries on "comfortable collaboration" (p. 55) as worthy of further study. A group that chooses to work on an initiative but not extend that to the classroom, or a group that chooses to limit inquiries into classroom instructional practices, may be seeking to keep the tough questions off their agenda. "Major elements of the prevailing norms of privacy are left intact" (p. 55). For collaboration to be effective and go beyond the advice-giving, material-sharing stage to seeking fundamental change, Fullan and Hargreaves hold that groups must focus on reflective inquiry, joint work, and mutual observation. "Effective collaborations operate in the world of ideas, examining existing practices critically, seeking better alternatives and working hard together at bringing about improvements and assessing their worth" (p. 57).

John-Steiner et al. (1998) responded to a narrative presentation of teacher-researcher collaboration that was written in Readers Theater format. They looked critically at the emphasis on dialogue and responded that there exists a "lack of fairness and unequal power in some collaborations" (p. 775) and that there are situations where all collaborators are doing identical work. This same group asserted that the dialogue that Clark et al. (1996) documented in the narrative account of teacher-researcher collaboration needs to be linked to shared objectives, participants' values, and common work and pointed out that the result of dialogue in and of itself is not necessarily collaboration. A final criticism is that Clark et al. described the teachers' feeling of improved relationships and mutual support among teachers but did not shed light on "direct evidence that a diminished sense of isolation contributes to more effective teaching or to reduced drop out from teaching" (p. 779). John-Steiner et al. conclude that building a theory of collaboration will necessitate specifying multiple definitions and multiple models of collaborative practice.

Leonard and Leonard (1999) recognize that in order to both create and sustain a culture of professional collaboration, a new understanding of "appropriate school leadership" (p. 237) is required. Although their study upheld the pivotal role of the principal in school improvement initiatives, all the schools reported that "professionally oriented schools must be characterized by various forms of leadership and by participative decision-making processes and structures" (p. 239). Their study supported the value of the informal culture of the school. They found that scheduled meetings and forced membership in groups could backfire. Enthusiasm aside, administrators have to take care to not formalize the life out of professional collaboration. They recommend allowing room for opportunities so that collaboration in its "purest form" can remain spontaneous, voluntary, and grounded in shared goals and commitment.

LEADERSHIP IN COLLABORATIVE MODELS

Recent collaboration studies that are based in organizational dynamics focus on the roles of the collaborators as leaders (Winer & Ray, 1994; Kouzes & Posner, 1995; Rubin, 1998). These collaborations involve larger numbers of persons often representing distinct organizations. There is a distinction made among cooperative relationships, coordinated efforts, and collaboration. Time frame, formality, mission, structure, and planning are some of the elements that distinguish different types of joint efforts in organizational collaboration. Factors that are necessary for successful collaboration include environment, group membership characteristics, organizational structures, communication, purpose, and resources (Mattessich & Monsey, 1992).

In *The Leadership Challenge* Kouzes and Posner (1995) write that collaboration now has a place among the many "processes for achieving and sustaining high performance. . . . The increasing emphasis on re-engineering, world-class quality, knowledge work, and electronic communication, along with the surging number of global alliances and local partnerships, is testimony to the fact that in a more complex, wired world, the winning strategies will be based upon the '*we* not *I*' philosophy" (p. 152). Their research showed that every extraordinary achievement was accomplished by many people, not just one. In addition to their original 550 cases, thousands of stories from business organizations around the world attest to the belief that the team effort is the best chance for a successful outcome. Leaders who foster collaboration were seen as more personally credible than those who believed that competition was a better choice of methods to achieve success.

DePree (1992) draws parallels between institutional leaders and jazz musicians. There is a balance of playing solo and playing as a member of a group. The leader is dependent on the group, has to trust the musicians, and must stay confident that the unpredictability will add to the performance. This improvisation results in music that would be impossible for any one musician or for a traditional musical group. In *Collaboration Skills for Educators and Nonprofit Leaders* Rubin (1998) refers to DePree's analogy to make the point that collaboration skills can be learned. He considers musicians who learn to play an instrument, play together with a group, and serve as leaders learn "the strength and weaknesses of their musical partners, all so that they might improvise together" (p. 40).

DePree's analogy precisely defines the manner of collaboration that best serves the academic needs of our students. Working with our strengths we bring to the collaboration that which only we have to share. Together, what comes of the collaboration is then a whole that is greater than the sum of its parts. No other joint effort in education can bring two professionals together to create more than they could have created alone—not compromise, coordination, or cooperation. Goal-oriented collaboration within the school not only changes the way we work to improve education, it changes the way we think about ourselves as learners. It is this fundamental realization that can have the greatest impact on our schools that operate within the constructivist theory of knowledge building (Brooks & Brooks, 1993; Steffe & Gale, 1995).

Teachers who collaborate report that it is the dialogue of the group that gives them a sense of freedom (Miller, 1990). Within the group, change is tangible, possibilities are exciting, and the energy to teach is revitalized. Collaborative work can be uncomfortable (Duckworth, 1997) for a group that asks hard, fundamental questions. The members of the group must have a commitment to reflective inquiry. In *Who Will Save Our Schools? Teachers as Constructivist Leaders* Lambert et al. (1997) argue that it is the reflective process that builds the capacity for leadership and change. "And because learning is social rather than solitary, teachers who are learners actively participate in the conversations that lead to learning and thus to change" (p. 157). Teachers who participate in research groups go through different types of changes in relation to their teaching. They may change their view of how to teach and their view of "how knowledge about teaching is developed, understood, and communicated to others" (Elmore, Peterson, & McCarthey, 1996, p. 243). Fullan and Hargreaves (1996; revised edition) urge teachers to become

Serendipity

The reason leaders may seek out collaborative experiences is because they are confident of their own knowledge, not threatened by the expertise of colleagues, risk-takers and avid learners, insatiably curious, and delighted by serendipity. They also are easily bored by routine.

–Policymaker

"impassioned moral change agents" who will fight for school improvement in the future, a future they see as one "in which the learning of teachers will become inextricably bound to the learning of those they teach" (p. xiii).

Attempting to change school culture incurs risks, and the educators who venture into uncharted territory realize that the journey may be bumpy and they could end up right where they started (surrounded by smug naysayers, no doubt). In his personal memoir of collaborating for change in a public suburban high school English department, Larson (1997) reflects that his greatest fear is that all of his pleas for conversation with his colleagues will result in his isolation. He fears that alienation will land him back in his classroom, alone. He concludes his memoir by quoting Greene (1988):

> And that won't do. "The aim," according to Maxine Greene, "is to find (or create) an authentic public space . . . one in which diverse human beings can appear before one another as to quote Hannah Arendt, 'the best they know how to be.' I want to cultivate, in the full view and with the help of my colleagues, "a consciousness . . ." as Greene says, "of what *ought* to be, from a moral and ethical point of view, and what is in the making, what *might* be in an always open world" (1988, p. xi). For this, I require and will continue to insist upon an honest, probing, fearless, and ongoing exchange with my colleagues, my administrators, and my students (pp. 116-117).

CHAPTER 3

The Teaching Profession

There are many viewpoints to consider when we try to understand the complexity of a working relationship. A concept like collaboration that manifests itself as a part of this relationship does not exist in a vacuum. We are working in schools in our various roles, each with unwritten rules of protocol. Educators do not just appear one day at a school and say, Here we are—let's collaborate. We are products of the professional educational process we have undergone. We are players in the school environment within which we teach and work. We live in this society that is undergoing an information revolution that is having a widespread impact on teaching and learning. And we stand on the shoulders of many giants who have studied the phenomenon of collaboration in education, business, and the nonprofit arenas. The challenge is in knowing not what to include in the effort to put collaboration within a larger context that is relevant to you, the reader, but what to exclude. Be choosy. Use the research as it relates to your work and to your vision.

The following sections touch on other areas of education research that are relevant to this study of collaboration. Their examination is essential because some studies (for example, in the culture of teaching) may convince the reader that collaboration among educators from varying cultural biases within education is an insurmountable goal. Seeking out these divergent views on this subject and delving into each area are risks that are necessary for you to have the big picture surrounding this issue. There is comfort in acknowledging the body of literature that surrounds collaboration and bringing to the reader those points that may seem contentious and insurmountable. In this way, together we can discover the strengths and weaknesses of the framework of collaboration that is at the heart of this book. Without a careful investigation of each of the following areas of study, we might float around without the fundamental structures we need to lay a solid foundation for collaboration among educators in the schools.

Each of the following sections highlights an area of study relevant to collaboration. The sections included in this chapter are as follows: "The Culture of Teaching," "Teacher Education," and "Societal Influences on Education." Within the first two sections the arrangement of topics addressed is approximately chronological. This arrangement is used to aid you in following the progression of a particular area of study over time. Contrary to appearances, the goal is not to provide a complete historical background in each topic of study, but the selective coverage should serve as a useful guide. The remaining section focuses on current trends that impact education today.

THE CULTURE OF TEACHING

Historically, the culture of teaching has been described primarily as a culture of isolation and autonomy. The image of the teacher closing the door of the classroom is a lasting one. This traditional view of the "egg crate school" (Lortie, 1975, p. 15) has deep roots. In his 1932 classic study, *The Sociology of Teaching,* Waller tells of the "keen and often bitter" (p. 429) rivalry between teachers who vie for the same limited benefits and rewards. He describes the relationship of the teacher to his colleagues: "Teachers are a closed group, a dominant group, with the morality of the dominant group; yet they are engaged in rivalry, and are cut off from contact with each other by that rivalry; the school-teacher stereotype cuts down yet further their intimacy with each other, while it throws them back upon each other for company; close association in their work throws them into constant contact, but the restrictions imposed by the situation prevent the completeness of intimacy" (p. 428). It is this paradox within the culture of teaching that Waller identifies: "Rivalry, which cuts teachers off from each other, and the constant hunger for shop talk, which brings them together, are distinctive features of the society of school teachers" (p. 430).

Even today a part of the teacher folklore is the bemoaning of the fact that their students were unprepared by previous teachers. Of course, they lament with their fellow teachers about other fellow teachers. Waller found "shop talk" to be one of the wholesome and hopeful things about the profession. However, he also noted that the exclusivity of discussing teaching ad infinitum led to a personal degeneration called "the reduction of personality" (p. 431). It is the narrowing of the attentional field from the greater mental universe to living, breathing, and dreaming teaching that is so dangerous to the balance of the well-rounded teacher. Teachers must struggle to be "whole" persons with interests outside of education so that in their role as teachers, they can educate the whole child.

The destructive professional loneliness of the beginning teacher is described in *The Real World of the Beginning Teacher* (National Commission on Teacher Education and Professional Standards, 1966). After a theory-based preparation and inadequately designed student teacher program, beginning teachers are thrust into a situational sink-or-swim reality. With no established forum for teacher dialogue, a new teacher may feel that the veteran teachers will view entering into a collaborative relationship as a sign of weakness. The impressions they get from the veteran teachers are that they should be able to make it on their own. The first year of teaching has the aura of an initiation rite of passage. In *Life in Classrooms* Jackson's (1968) view of the closed door is that teachers close it to eliminate the possibility of unsolicited inspections. He found that teachers did have a desire to draw more heavily on the services of other specialists within the system (in elementary schools this includes art, music, and drama teachers), while at the same time wanting to preserve the feeling of being on their own in the classroom.

The most authoritative study to date on the subject of the culture of teaching is *Schoolteacher: A Sociological Study* (Lortie, 1975). Lortie follows Waller's lead in placing great emphasis on the importance of social insight. His goal in this study was to document genuine insights into the nature of teaching as an occupation. Lortie coined the phrase "egg crate school," which refers to a type of organization wherein "each teacher was assigned specific areas of responsibility and was expected to teach students the stipulated knowledge and skills without assistance from others" (p. 15). Lortie foresaw the persistence of separation and low task interdependence in American schools. One of the major shifts from Waller's study to Lortie's publication was the gender under scrutiny. Waller's teachers were almost exclusively males and Lortie's subjects were primarily females. That shift reflected the popularization of "work outside the home" during the time that Lortie documented his study (late 1960s and early 1970s). Lortie explored the connection between independence and high turnover from the employment viewpoint. Task interdependence would have required that teachers find and accept interpersonal relationships within the school. The organizational system of the school was designed to absorb the comings and goings of teachers every school year. This reliance on independence of effort makes perfect sense from an administrative vantage point.

Lortie discusses the need for trust in a collegial relationship in his chapter "Speculations on Change." Since teacher individualism and self-selection are still dominant, an environment of trust is not common. Lortie compares the demands of teacher education programs and medical school programs. Medical school program demands on students are so great as to require students to band together and rely on each other for successful matriculation. No such demands are made on preservice educators. There is no "shared ordeal" (p. 237) in most, if not all, education programs. Lortie points to the "softness" of the curricula, stating that "people in schools of education who favor greater teacher collegiality might consider making sterner demands on their students" (p. 237).

Other factors identified by Lortie as responsible for perpetuating teacher isolation (and intellectual narrowness) include the cellular organization of schools, the lack of a mutual technical language, teaching as a "private ordeal," self-doubt, preference for boundedness, limited opportunities for mutual consultation during the working day, and contact between teachers and other educators having a peripheral status as compared to their major obligations. Lortie calls for greater adaptability, more effective colleague relationships, and more sharing of practitioner knowledge and expertise. He predicted the strains between the historical ethos of teachers and the demands of the new situation produced by the erosion of tradition.

> **Relationship Rides**
>
> The relationships that are most fruitful in collaborations are NOT smooth rides of agreement and no conflict for participants but just the opposite. They are collaborative when there is safety and respect for differences and the skills to cultivate and use differences for the benefit of all involved.—*Teacher Educator*

When he worked with school personnel in staff development situations, Sarason (1983/1995) asked the participants to think of two instances in their lives where interest was kindled to such an extent that the experience was truly formative. After the participants shared their answers, Sarason would ask, "How frequently have you had experiences in school as a teacher that were interesting?" (p. 205). He describes their response as anxious laughter. Sarason summarizes the discussion that followed his question with three points. First, there is a low frequency of interesting experiences in school as a teacher. Second, the organization of the school makes it less likely for interesting experiences to occur. Third, and most pertinent to our topic of educator collaboration, schoolteachers are too isolated from each other and the outside world within the classroom structure. The organization of the school and the isolation of the classroom do not provide the social contexts from which interesting experiences emerge.

Goodlad (1984), in *A Place Called School: Prospects for the Future,* found that "teacher-to-teacher links" (p. 187) for mutual assistance in teaching or collaborative school improvement were weak or nonexistent, especially in the secondary schools. As for teachers using resource educators, he found that teachers drew upon them "only a little and said that they were of limited value" (p. 187). Goodlad's study included approximately 27,000 participants. His data showed that three-quarters of the sample (at all levels of schooling) would like to observe other teachers at work.

 21

They did not feel that they knew their fellow teachers, how they behaved with students, their educational beliefs, or their competence. The same amount of teachers, 76 percent, reported that they had the right amount of autonomy in their classrooms (p. 189). Overall, teachers felt a decreasing sense of powerfulness as the focus moved from the classroom to the school as a whole. Their perception of power resides in decisions that impact their students but not themselves. In contrast to the teachers' perceptions, principals perceived teachers as more powerful and involved in the decision-making process than the teachers perceived themselves to be (p. 191).

The same year that Goodlad introduced us to *A Place Called School*, Sizer (1984) published his first volume in the study of high schools and introduced us to Horace Smith, a fictional high school teacher who represents a compilation of many teachers. Sizer highlights the paradox of teachers feeling both committed to their vocation and demoralized by it. He describes a typical teacher as an idealist who genuinely wants students to succeed but is nevertheless vulnerable when minimal conditions for good teaching (such as attendance) are not supported. This vulnerability leads to a lessening of self-confidence. Sizer found that students like self-confident teachers who have the courage to use silence and patience constructively. "Confident teachers create confidence in their students" (p. 183). Although teachers are given autonomy in the classroom, Sizer reports that the teacher lacks "respect-laden autonomy enjoyed by other professionals" (p. 184). The rules and regulations governing the classroom are handed down to the teachers without any consultation. Teachers, therefore, lack any sense of ownership, "a sense among the teachers working together that the school is theirs, and that its future and their reputation are indistinguishable" (p. 184).

In the chapter written by Feiman-Nemser and Floden (1986) entitled "The Cultures of Teaching" in the third edition of the *Handbook of Research on Teaching*, a general discussion is presented related to teacher interactions with administrators, students, other teachers, and parents. However, no mention is made of the interactions taking place with other professionals in the school who are skilled and knowledgeable in teacher collaboration. The discussion about interactions with other teachers is rather blunt, suggesting that "teachers have peers but no colleagues" (p. 508). The authors report studies that show that some teachers think that they would benefit from more collegial interactions than are currently available in most schools. They mention the fear of revealing areas of weakness in classroom instructional practice.

In "Teacher Isolation and the New Reform," Flinders (1988) considered the isolation of the teaching profession as a paradox. Although teaching is a lonely profession (Sarason, 1966), Flinders describes classrooms as crowded places in which to carry on one's daily work. He cites

Enormous Risks

Collaboration, like most good ideas in education, is easier said than done. There are enormous risks and frequent costs associated with observing, communicating, sharing knowledge, and being able to talk openly about the work we do. The risks and costs of sustaining a climate of working in isolation, in opposite corners of the sandbox, are far more detrimental to our schools.–*Administrator*

secondary teachers in particular, who often see an average of 120 students per day. Flinders also finds that the long-term effects of isolation undermine the instructional quality that isolation, viewed as a work strategy, is intended to protect. He sees isolation as a barrier to professional development and school reform. Initial reforms that dealt with isolation focused on staff development activities that attempted to train teachers in interpersonal communication and social competence. Self-improvement activities increase the demand on teachers' time and are viewed as another threat to professional survival. Later reform proposals such as peer coaching and teacher mentoring represent a blend of organizational and teacher-oriented perspectives.

According to Rosenholtz (1989), teachers' productive contributions are a direct function of the professional fulfillment teachers derive from their work. In *Teachers' Workplace: The Social Organization of Schools,* her conceptual argument (and quantitative analysis) identified three conditions necessary for such fulfillment. The first is the teachers' autonomy and discretion—the sense that achieving work goals results directly from purposive actions, or teachers' feeling that their own intentional efforts cause positive changes to occur. The second condition deals with teachers' psychic rewards. If teachers' rewards do not outweigh their frustrations, particularly in their relationships with students, work tends to lose its meaning and alienation increases. The final condition is learning opportunities, opportunities to increase one's talents and instructional strategies to better master one's environment, to repel professional stagnation, and to experience a sense of continuous progress and intellectual growth.

Rosenholtz claims that teachers' terminal boredom, the loss of their original meaning, their overwhelming sense of unappreciation, and their lack of professional empowerment results in "stuck" schools, and it costs these schools dearly: "They usurp teachers' capacity to dream" (p. 165). Teachers' sense of commitment was suffocated without learning opportunities, task autonomy, and psychic rewards. Stuck teachers lack passion for teaching, and that "makes them passively suffer until the current storm, whatever its point of departure" (p. 164), passes. They lose faith in themselves as teachers and contributing members of society. They lose the motivation to muster the energy needed to go the extra mile for the betterment of their students.

Little (1990) feels strongly that long-standing occupational and organizational traditions buttress teaching as a private endeavor. She finds

this to be in conflict with teachers being "pressed, invited, and cajoled into ventures in 'collaboration'" (p. 530). In "The Persistence of Privacy: Autonomy and Initiative in Teachers' Professional Relations," Little describes school teaching as an "assemblage of entrepreneurial individuals whose autonomy is grounded in norms of privacy and noninterference and is sustained by the very organization of teaching work" (p. 530). She contends that the culture that Lortie identified as individualistic, conservative, and present-oriented is not only unaltered but is perpetuated by many instances of teacher collaboration or exchange. The forces that steer teachers toward collective interactions seem powerless against the school's fundamental purposes or the implications of the patterns of practice that have accumulated over time. Referring to Lortie again, Little suggests that the reluctance toward involvement in any collective teacher group stems from fears that such involvement might expose the teachers' autonomic classroom activities to criticism and conflict.

In tracing the history of teaching in America from 1890 to 1990, Cuban (1998) identifies four (of six) explanations for "how teachers teach" that explain why teacher-centered instruction endured including the environment (cultural inheritance and social functions of schools); the organizational (implementation of policies and the structures of schooling); occupational socialization (the nature of teaching, who enters the occupation, and future teachers' long apprenticeship of observing their elders); and the individual whose knowledge and beliefs shape classroom behavior. The remaining two arguments, which suggest reasons why classroom changes may have occurred, include occasional implementation of classroom reform policies and teachers' knowledge and beliefs. Cuban does see gradual steps toward incorporating student-centeredness even from the bastion of classroom autonomy, the elementary teachers. He predicts the steady growth of "hybrid versions" (p. 277) of teacher-centeredness and student-centeredness.

The implications of Cuban's findings highlight the fact that teachers have been dealing with the same old issues vis-à-vis their classrooms for the last century. Also, teachers are leaders in their classrooms, and that knowledge should encourage them. And finally, Cuban's results should convince practitioners that school

Layering Effect

With collaboration, more content may be covered by "layering" assignments. Students have one project for three subjects, which lowers stress for teachers and students and allows for more time to produce quality work. The reinforcement of the subject matter from different perspectives strengthens the concept learned by the student. Teachers can cover their own curricula while providing a content-rich unit that will not only engage students for the present but will also stay with them for the long term.–*Practitioner*

reform talk does apply to them, not just to the state or district level, and that the choices they have at the classroom level are situationally constrained. Teachers need to work collaboratively to lessen the organizational constraints on their autonomy within the classroom and thereby create more opportunities for change in their schools.

In his chapter, "Beginning Again: The Mystery of Teaching," Ayers (1993) calls teaching the "vocation of vocations" (p. 127). He writes lyrically that "teaching begins in challenge and is never far from mystery" (p. 127). More important than the range of practitioner knowledge and skills necessary to do the job, teaching requires a thoughtful, caring person at its center. In her memoir about her life as a teacher, Tomkins (1996) reminisces about her days as a schoolgirl: "The teachers who made the most difference to me were the ones who loved their subjects and didn't hide it" (p. 61). Tomkins learned from those passionate teachers that you could love something with your body and your heart as well as your mind. She was inspired by this type of teaching, teaching that gave her permission to express her "unbounded enthusiasm" (p. 61).

According to Ayers (1993), teaching depends on growth and development. It is replete with dynamic situations that present opportunities for insights, understandings, and intellectual puzzles. In order to be actively present for all that teaching offers, teachers must stay alive. They must own who they are as a person and as a learner if they want to be able to teach others. Ayers describes teaching as "often isolated and isolating, and an assumption of teacher preparation is that it must always be this way" (p. 131). He recommends that teachers find allies, supporters, and friends and build alliances that can be lifesaving. Ayers quotes Jane Addams's question, "How shall we respond to the dreams of youth?" and calls this a "teacher's kind of question" (p. 139). I suggest that we twist the question a bit and give teachers a renewed chance to dream as we ask, *How shall we respond to the dreams of teachers?*

TEACHER EDUCATION

In his major study, *The Sociology of Teaching,* Waller (1932) starts his preface and ends his book discussing the social nature of the school. His preface begins, "What this book tells us is what every teacher knows, that the world of school is a social world. Those human beings who live together in the school, though deeply severed in one sense, nevertheless spin a tangled web of interrelationships; that web and the people in it make up the social world of school" (p. v). He concludes his book by offering the following recommendation for teacher education: "A central point of the teacher's training, then, should be the attempt to give him insight into the nature of the social reality which is the school. . . .

Prospective teachers learn all the new educational theories while they are in school, but they must learn how to teach from horny-handed men who have been teaching a long time" (p. 459).

Sixty-five years later, Bean (1997) reports that regardless of the strategies taught to preservice educators in their teacher education programs, the dominant influence is the cooperating teacher. The preservice teachers Bean studied carefully checked the climate they felt the cooperating teacher wanted to maintain. Throughout the study of teacher education programs, we will see the major influence of the cooperating and supervising teachers over the content of the education curriculum.

> ### Against Prevailing Norms
>
> Just putting the "process" of collaboration into place–opportunities for teachers to discuss their practice, observe each other, and work in teams to design curriculum–is not enough. Too often these attempts are met with disinterest or even resistance because, really, collaboration is tough–it involves a lot of time, and it goes against prevailing norms of autonomy.–*Policymaker*

Teacher education programs can't seem to catch a break. In 1963, Koerner frankly claims that "course work in education deserves its ill repute. It is moot, often puerile, repetitious, dull and ambiguous—incontestably. Two factors make it this way: the limitations of the instructor and the limitations of the subject matter that has been remorselessly fragmented, subdivided, and inflated, and in many cases was not adequate in its uninflated state" (p. 18). Those who studied the education of American teachers found that there was minimal consistency among teacher education programs (Conant, 1963; Peck & Tucker, 1973; Cruickshank, 1984). One of the recurrent differences among programs is the balance that they place between the general education courses and the professional courses geared toward preparing future teachers. The overlap of those areas was also a concern. Some believe that the learning theories taught in general and educational psychology courses were duplicated in professional education classes and were thereby redundant and wasteful.

In their "Research on Teacher Education" report in the *Second Handbook of Research on Teaching,* Peck and Tucker (1973) conclude that "teacher education can no longer remain in a happily ignorant, ineffectual state consisting of romanticized lectures, on the one hand, and fuzzy or unplanned 'practical' experience on the other" (p. 971). They predicted that the day would not be far off that there would be a performance-based system for the certification of teachers and, more importantly, the establishment of an effective system of continuing education for all members of the teaching profession who seek lifelong professional development.

The 1980s were a major decade in the American teacher education reform movement. The National Commission on Excellence in

Education published *A Nation at Risk* in 1983. The Holmes Group and the Carnegie Task Force on Teaching as a Profession both issued their first reports in 1986. This confluence of reports proposed many changes in teacher education, including "the ways that teacher education students are recruited and selected and in the content, organization, and control of teacher education programs" (Zeichner, Melnick, & Gomez, 1996, p. 1). The major teacher unions, consortia of teacher education programs, major professional teacher organizations, state departments of education, and leading teacher educators all added their perspectives on the subject of teacher education reform. It was at this time that the professional development school (PDS) became identified as a functioning, exemplary, public school that had three major functions: student achievement, teacher induction, and improvement of practice (Holmes Group, 1986). These schools were models of collaboration between school districts, universities, and, sometimes, teachers unions. At these schools, practitioners, researchers, and clinical faculty collaborate to both expand the knowledge base and prepare preservice educators (Abdal-Haqq, 1992).

In 1982, the National Education Association (NEA) published *Excellence in Our Schools: Teacher Education: An Action Plan*. This report indicates that the three major functions of teaching are facilitating learning, managing the classroom, and making professional decisions. Professional decision making occurs across as well as in the context of the other two functions (Cruickshank, 1996). There is very little evidence in the sources describing teacher education programs that speaks to the explicit instruction in professional decision making for teachers.

Ten years later, in 1992, the NEA sponsored a monograph entitled *Excellence in Teacher Education: Helping Teachers Develop Learner-Centered Schools* as a part of their School Restructuring Series (Darling-Hammond, Griffin, & Wise). According to this monograph, the future of teacher education revolves around three major issues: the content of teacher education programs with a focus on the kind of teachers and teaching required in the schools of the future,the context of the programs to ensure exemplary practice, and public policy issues that impact on the schools of the future. Any school restructuring would require changes in teacher education. This publication focuses on the restructuring of schools from teacher-centered to the creation of learner-centered schools and the changing view of teaching that in turn requires the restructuring, or reform, of teacher education. A fundamental change in philosophy is indicated: "Teachers must be asked and expected to 'do the right things,' rather than to 'do things right'" (Darling-Hammond, Griffin, & Wise, 1992, p. 9).

Once the teacher education conversation began to incorporate the learner-centered viewpoint, it was clear that changes were coming. In order for teachers to adapt to understanding the cultural and social contexts of their students' learning, they needed to begin to consider rethinking their own contexts of learning. This content would then be added to the already overloaded teacher education curriculum.

Concerns about the lack of agreement among experts as to what constitutes a fundamental program of teacher education (Conant, 1963; Peck & Tucker, 1973; Cruickshank, 1984) continue to persist (Cruickshank, 1996). This simple but obstinate stumbling block, while accepted in education, is uncommon in most professional programs of study. Another obstacle noted by Cruickshank includes the completion of the program within the context of the undergraduate degree (unlike other professional schools that require at least one year of graduate study). This issue has many difficulties associated with it, including the already mentioned lack of consensus on a standard curriculum, economic hardships that will not be alleviated by the future teachers' salaries, and the prolonged separation between preservice and professional development education. Cruickshank (1996) comprehensively describes twenty-nine teacher education reform proposals and six "promising approaches" (p. 101). He includes a litany of criticisms from within the ranks of teacher educators, including such concerns as "teacher educators cannot explain why they are doing what they are doing; preservice teachers do not learn how to be reflective; teacher educators do not model a variety of teaching techniques; and teacher educators avoid discussing teaching and the preparation curriculum" (p. 133). Cruickshank concludes, "We never have lacked ideas for the reform of teacher preparation, but we have sorely lacked the consensus, focus, moxie, and persistence to carry them through" (p. 133).

Magic

Time is an essential component but by itself does not create an atmosphere that supports collaboration. A lot of districts imagine that collaboration will magically happen when more teachers have the same prep hours.

—Practitioner

When Clandinin, Davies, Hogan, and Kennard (1993) edited *Learning to Teach, Teaching to Learn: Stories of Collaboration in Teacher Education*, they focused on narrative inquiry as an expression of teachers' practical knowledge. They consider theoretical knowledge to be a part of teachers' knowledge that is constructed and reconstructed in practice and through reflection in practice. They emphasize teacher education as a collaborative inquiry where the collaboration is essential between student teachers, university (supervisory) partners, and cooperating teachers. Their view of teaching preservice educators was not the traditional transmission of information but collaborative inquiry involving the students and teachers. Clandinin et al. refer to Schön's (1987) reflective practices to enrich the collaborative experience. They stipulate that collaborative inquiry occurs in the practice of teaching through Schön's process of both reflection-in- and reflection-on-practice. Overall, they are seeking to create a middle ground for

teacher education between the school and the university. They conclude that it is in this new space that personal connections would help educators be more thoughtful. That thoughtfulness would then reflect on their experiences with their students.

In a way, Munby and Russell (1996) are also seeking a middle ground in teacher education, but their goal is to establish a "healthy interaction of theory and practice" (p. 1). In their paper presented at the American Educational Research Association conference in New York, they explored the precedence in teacher education of "theory" (university courses) preceding "practice" (clinical experiences in schools). They argue that the status quo operates on an outmoded and incorrect view of the epistemology of practice. Their premise has three major points: a historical view of teacher education, an epistemological view centered around Schön's approach to the nature of practical knowledge, and an empirical view based on data from a group of preservice educators. They conclude, on the basis of their three-point argument, that theory should follow significant practice, both in learning to teach and in research on teaching, and that perhaps the productive interaction of theory and practice could finally be achieved in the profession of teaching and the practice of teacher education.

The focus in teacher education reform in the 1990s included reflective practice, a strong push toward regulation and national standards in teacher education programs, and preparing teachers appropriately for diversity (Zeichner, Melnick, & Gomez, 1996). Cries for regulatory accreditation are heard over the laments about weak and unbalanced programs, conflicting and overlapping state and national standards, and political self-interest. In *A License to Teach: Raising Standards for Teaching*, Darling-Hammond, Wise, and Klein (1999) describe the Minnesota Board of Teaching experience as an exemplar in current teacher education reform at the state level. The authors strongly suggest that "a meaningful license to teach will be crucial for ensuring that teachers have the knowledge they need as a foundation for twenty-first-century schools" (p. ix).

Again, in *The Right to Learn: A Blueprint for Creating Schools That Work*, Darling-Hammond (1997) highlights what teachers need to know and be able to do. She claims that teachers need to know about collaboration so that their students can experience shared learning, so that teachers can collaborate with other teachers, and so that teachers can work with parents as partners in their children's educational experiences at home and at school. Arthur E. Wise, president of one of the two major American teacher education organizations, the National Council for Accreditation of Teacher Education (NCATE), testified before the Senate Committee on Labor and Human Resources in May 1998. In his testimony, entitled "Assuring Quality for the Nation's Teachers," Wise encouraged all institutions that prepare teachers to meet nationally recognized

 29

professional standards for accreditation. He proclaimed that meeting those standards is the teaching profession's long-range goal.

In all of the educational arenas represented by resource educators (special education, reading specialists, school library media specialists, etc.), there are new standards and principles which point to the need for the development of a collaborative theoretical framework for teacher educators and professional development specialists within the schools. Teacher educators are slowly adjusting to the new Interstate New Teacher Assessment and Support Consortium (INTASC) standards, which were sponsored by the Council of Chief State School Officers (CCSSO) (Darling-Hammond, Wise, & Klein, 1999). These standards "represent a common core of teaching knowledge and skills which will help all students acquire 21st century knowledge and skills. The standards were developed to be compatible with the advanced certification standards of the new National Board for Professional Teaching Standards" (INTASC, 1992, p. 1). There are ten principles included in the standards. Of those ten, the teacher collaborating with other school educators to achieve the goals as stated would best serve six principles. For example, in Principle 4, the teacher understands and uses a variety of instructional strategies to encourage students' development of critical thinking, problem solving, and performance skills. The goals as stated in this principle could perhaps best be achieved by the teacher collaborating with the school librarian to include technology (the software program *Inspiration* would be applicable here) or the reading specialist to use reading strategies for problem solving.

Embrace the Innovation

There is often a belief by some enthusiasts that one must embrace the innovation 100 percent of the time for all things and all reasons. This, of course, dissuades many from ever trying something new.–*Teacher Educator*

Many new national educational standards have been published during the past few years. Both the reading specialist profession and school library field revised their standards. *Standards for Reading Professionals: A Reference for the Preparation of Educators in the United States* (International Reading Association [IRA], 1998) includes the following objective under the description of the role of specialized reading professional: "works cooperatively and collaborates with other professionals in planning programs to meet the needs of a diverse population of learners" (p. 5). In *Information Power: Building Partnerships for Learning,* which includes *Information Power: The Nine Information Literacy Standards for Student Learning* (American Association of School Librarians and Association for Educational Communications and Technology, 1998b), goals are stated that ensure that school librarians collaborate with teachers for student learning. In a chapter devoted to collaboration, leadership, and technology, collaboration is identified as a key theme in building partnerships for learning.

The Council for Exceptional Children, which is the organization that encompasses special education resource educators, states in their mission that "We believe . . . special education professionals have knowledge and skills to share with other professionals to meet the diverse learning needs of individuals with exceptionalities" (1998, p. 1).

With the advent of all these advances in teacher standards, one might wonder where these national organizations get their knowledge base. According to Zeichner (1999), neither policymakers nor teacher educators heed teacher education research. Writing in his article, "The New Scholarship in Teacher Education," Zeichner contends that this concern is not just an American dilemma. So, although he sees great advances in teacher education research, Zeichner does not connect the dots to the advances related to establishing and enforcing teacher standards from the national organizations mentioned above.

Locally, state departments of education are graded on a variety of criteria by *Education Week*. The Illinois State Board of Education (ISBE) Professional Development Framework adopted strategies for improving the professional preparation and continuing professional development of teachers in 1996. Recommendation 1 states that teacher preparation programs should be redesigned around state board identified standards. One of those identified standards includes preparation for collaboration with colleagues and parents (ISBE, 1998). Illinois has good reason to revisit strategies for preparing teachers and ensuring professional development. According to *Quality Counts 2000, Education Week*'s fourth annual state-by-state look at public schooling, Illinois deserves a "C" for failing on promises to put better teachers in our classrooms, a "C+" on standards and accountability, and a "D+" on improving teacher quality (2000, Section 1, p. 20).

In contrast to Illinois, Connecticut stood out as an exemplary program, where prospective teachers must pass rigorous certification examinations and subject mastery tests. First-year teachers are assigned mentors, and teachers must renew their certification every five years by proving that they are involved in continuing professional development courses. While the powers that be at the state board of education attempt to improve teacher education in Illinois, the *Chicago Tribune* reported on January 10, 2000, that (then) Secretary of Education Richard Riley stated that because teacher requirements are changing, most instructors are feeling "ill-prepared" for the classroom. Riley recommended that the pressing needs of American schools are to upgrade "preparation, induction, mentoring, support, professional development and pay" (Section 1, p. 10) of teachers. Following Secretary Riley's advice to upgrade aspects

 31

of the vocation of teaching necessitates an understanding of the societal influences that are impacting our schools today.

SOCIETAL INFLUENCES ON EDUCATION

This new age that is before us beholds unimaginable heights and lamentable restraints. It is a time of great change for many and a time of being left behind for others. The social realities of our time necessitate a re-evaluation of the role of the classroom teacher and resource educator in the school. In fact, some social critics sound the death knell for public education (Postman, 1995). In *The End of Education*, Postman points the finger back at the American culture that is not "presently organized to promote the idea of childhood; and without that idea schooling loses much of its point" (p. 196). He does not state this flippantly. In fact, he bemoans this reality since he sees the public school as creating the public, and he does not see how that would happen without public schooling. And, indeed, if we lose the meaning of childhood, then what is the meaning of adulthood in America?

Meier (1995) is committed to public education because it feeds into her faith in democracy as the best chance for our children's futures. In *The Power of Their Ideas: Lessons for America from a Small School in Harlem*, Meier acknowledges the soft underbelly of democracy's promise of public education. And still Meier writes that dealing with the complicated is what training for good citizenship is all about. "Ideas—the ways we organize knowledge—are the medium of exchange in democratic life" (p. 8). We are all the stronger for the clash of ideas, the differences among us. Meier sees the opportunity we have before us to reinvent our public schools as a way to use our power as a nation and perhaps rediscover ourselves in the process.

Gardner's (1999a) view is that education is at a crossroad. He writes in *The Disciplined Mind: What All Students Should Understand* that it is ironic that those nations that are currently deemed successful seem the most concerned about the unsuitability of their current schools for future needs. He contends that the differences in views about what the future holds are not relevant since there is a consensus that future schools and education will differ substantially from what we and our ancestors have known and, in most cases, taken for granted.

For a country to educate its citizenry to remain competitive in a rapidly changing world, the six major sets of trends identified by Gardner will require responses from leading educators (p. 42):

First, technological and scientific breakthroughs, led by the computer. Imaging technologies will help us learn more about our mental lives and how we learn.

Second, political trends that strain education as a system of values. This is a global issue especially in countries with changing political ecologies and even in America, where ultra-patriotic citizens embrace values that scare many of those who are considered to be underrepresented and marginalized in society. Future demographic trends foresee a shift from the majority. This shift will greatly impact our body politic.

Third, economic forces where the shift in economic growth leads to the knowledge society. More citizens will work in the service industry as providers of communication of knowledge in every industry. Knowledge then becomes the commodity of the future, where workers' job security will be based on how well they can learn and apply their knowledge base.

Fourth, the continued influence of the media on social, cultural, and personal trends. The global village exposes us to customs and moral visions of many different beliefs. The positive slant on this is that our sense of options is enlarged, and marginalization of minority groups becomes less likely. We will better know our cognitive lives through metacognition, multiple intelligences, and reflective thinking. This cognitive self-actualization will help lifelong learners who find themselves as adults needing to continue to learn either within one field or to change jobs. Adult learning will become a necessity for those in the job market.

Fifth, the shifting cartography of knowledge which makes it impossible to have a grasp on all the knowledge in any one field. It will be the skilled synthesizer, the one who can discriminate between information of value and irrelevant information, who will succeed. The interdisciplinary approach is another challenge to educators. In fact, the notion of functional literacy will be redefined. A new mix of literacies that include reading, visual, and auditory and an ability to reconfigure each as needed may prove to be the most useful.

Sixth, beyond modernism—postmodernism—multiculturalism approaches will challenge educators and need to be viewed differently from the K-12 and collegiate perspectives.

Indeed, his whole premise in *The Disciplined Mind* is based on what postmodernists would call a metanarrative, riddled with contradictions and fictions. Gardner feels that this trend should stay focused on collegiate education because postmodern perspectives need to be handled by mature students who have strong background knowledge in truth, beauty, and goodness. The multicultural stance that includes minorities and women in the canon poses its own challenges. Gardner questions the loosening of high standards in order to include works of lesser quality. Again, he contends that students need to develop a sense of high standards so that they become critical thinkers, prepared for a future with the best the past has to offer.

Books and articles abound that contain discussions related to education in the new millennium, in the twenty-first century, in this new information age. In *Education in a New Era,* editor Brandt (2000) emphasizes the impact on teachers since society seems fixated on the future, and the future is our business. This time period we are in does give one pause to reflect upon past achievements and trends and what the future might hold. Brandt makes two broad generalizations about the future: (1) technological change will continue at a rate difficult for people to keep pace with, and (2) technological changes will produce social, political, and economic changes that will demand responses from educational institutions. In fact, Brandt connects advances in technology (transportation, radio, and television) with enabling migration from developing nations to more developed areas and thereby producing educational responses such as multicultural and bilingual education. Other technological advances have made it medically possible for children to survive and, thus, require schooling. Many of these children might not have survived in days past. Moreover, changes in the workforce have changed our students' home lives, which creates new challenges for educators.

Of all the technological changes and resulting societal changes, it is the information revolution and all that the computer hath wrought that hits us with full force. The multimedia educational technology, the availability of vast quantities of information, the availability of e-mail for students, and the omnipresence of the Internet all have impacted the isolation of the classroom. Regardless of whether one considers the computer in education to be a panacea or a pariah, all agree that the digital divide has transformed the gulf between the "haves" and "have nots" in education into an abyss. This topic is discussed poignantly by Kozol in his 1991 publication, *Savage Inequalities: Children in America's Schools.* Noting the date, the reader will realize that the inequalities that Kozol researched pre-date the Internet, a major factor in the digital divide. Kozol's lament that children all start out wonderful and innocent and we "soil them needlessly" (p. 233) through the inequities in public education is a challenge to educators and policymakers to do what we can to level the playing field in America's schools.

> **Core and Necessary Concept**
>
> Collaboration is a core and necessary concept in the field of education, and skills in collaboration are necessary for effective teaching at all levels–in the preparation of teachers and their teaching of students.
> —*Teacher Educator*

The quest for educational equality has lasted since separate but equal schools were found to be unconstitutional almost fifty years ago. In "The Social Construction of Difference and the Quest for Educational Equality," Banks (in Brandt, 2000) adds that in more recent years we have seen the battle broaden to include the needs of children with limited English proficiency and children with special needs. Participants in the quest for educational equality include women, people of color, language minority groups, people with disabilities, people who live in rural areas, and people who are economically depressed. These voices are all helping to shape educational research, policy, and practice. Their efforts "uncovered—as well as contested—established paradigms, canons, categories, and concepts that they believed justified their marginalized status, defined them as the 'other,' and played a role in denying them equal educational opportunities" (p. 22).

An example of public schooling in suburban Chicago, Maine East High School draws from students who reside in Niles, Morton Grove, Des Plaines, Glenview, and Park Ridge. At Maine East High School, fifty-two languages are represented among the students (from more than seventy countries). The students who speak the English language as a mother tongue (28 percent) are in the minority (there are 2,200 students enrolled). This dramatic increase in students who read and speak English as a second language has led to the addition of the bilingual resource educator position in many schools. Students who may read English as a first language but who speak another language at home may need additional instruction in reading. The reading scores also suffer in many of our urban schools. At K-6 schools in the neighborhoods of Chicago where all students are natural English speakers (and they speak English at home), more than 80 percent of the students read below grade level.

In *Collaboration: A Success Strategy for Special Educators,* Cramer (1998) traces the significant changes in the field of special education to 1973 with the passage of P.L. 93-112, the Rehabilitation Act of 1973. Section 504 of the act was the first federal law to protect the civil rights of people with disabilities. Section 504 guaranteed that all educational institutions that had not previously accepted people with disabilities were now required to do so. This was just the beginning of the change that would take place in the next twenty-five years. Each successive public law has enhanced the special educator's role as collaborator. Several special education researchers, including Cramer, chronicle the diverse use of the collaborative process in special education literature (Johnson, Pugach, & Devlin, 1990; Winitzky et al., 1995; Gable & Manning, 1997; Hudson & Glomb, 1997). The field of special education began to meld consultation and collaboration in the 1990s. The Council for Exceptional Children (CEC) first published *What Every Special Educator Must Know* in 1995 (the third edition was published in 1998). The CEC sought input from teacher preparation programs and classroom teachers. The standardization that resulted includes several explicit descriptions of collaboration. A section focused entirely on knowledge demonstrates the centrality of collaboration in the special education field and skills related to communication and collaboration partnerships.

Steinberg (1996) writes in *Beyond the Classroom: Why School Reform Has Failed and What Parents Need to Do* that the major societal influence on education today is that students have changed over the last twenty-five years in the amount of engagement they have in school. Steinberg and his research team define engagement as "the degree to which students are psychologically 'connected' to what is going on in their classes" (p. 15). Using engagement as a barometer, Steinberg views it as an indicator of students' commitment "not only to education but to the goals and values held by adult society—by their parents, by their teachers, and by members of their community" (p. 16). He claims that years ago a teacher might have a few disengaged students, but today nearly half the students have "checked out" (p. 28). He finds that student disengagement is more pervasive and in some ways more harmful to our future than the other social problems involving youth such as crime, pregnancy, and violence.

Steinberg openly questions America's acknowledgment of this generation of underachieving students as a serious problem. By changing the way achievement is measured and assessed, schools (including colleges) have softened the look of the achievement decline. Steinberg sees this issue as "an achievement crisis of gargantuan proportions in this country" (p. 46). He sees this task as too large for school reformers to handle single-handedly; it will take a national effort involving schools, parents, employers, the media, and the students. The effort coming forth from educators could start by systematically exploring teaching and learning, thinking, and the constructivist approach in the classroom.

CHAPTER 4
Teaching and Learning

The current trends in education support the position of working together for the betterment of the students. These trends are a shift from the modernist role of the teacher in an isolated environment. The field of teacher education, while promoting the latest educational trends, does not offer preparation for the beginning teacher to learn how to collaborate with other educators. Indeed, consider (then) Secretary of Education Richard Riley's lament, as reported in the January 10, 2000, *Chicago Tribune*, that there are too few "talented, dedicated teachers" (Section 1, p. 10). Speaking to the National Conference on Teacher Quality, which was sponsored by the Education Department, Riley blamed much of the problem on the changing nature of teaching itself, "where teachers are expected to teach not only average pupils but also those with physical and emotional problems, hunger, language problems, and uninterested parents" (Section 1, p. 10).

In *Changing Teachers, Changing Times: Teachers' Work and Culture in the Postmodern Age,* Hargreaves (1994) looks at teachers and change as an ironic situation. He sees good-intentioned change devices failing where they are squeezed into the status quo. As for collaborative cultures in schools, he sees the likelihood for transformation into contrived collegiality. The fundamental problem is the confrontation of the increasingly postmodern world characterized by accelerating change, compression of time, cultural diversity, technological complexity, and globalization versus the modernistic school system that continues to pursue its outmoded purposes with static, inflexible structures.

Hargreaves's research is based on teachers' voices, which he found to be absent or used to merely echo the theories of educational researchers. Collaboration figures prominently in Hargreaves's work. He has real concerns about how collaborative cultures operate within the school. He sees them both as a burden as well as a blessing. "Well-intentioned drives to create collaborative cultures and to expunge the culture of teacher isolation and individualism from our schools are in serious danger of eliminating individuality among teachers, and with it the disagreeable creativity that can challenge administrative assumptions and be a powerful force for change" (1994, p. 17). Effective collaborative cultures tend to be spontaneous, voluntary, development-oriented, pervasive across time and space, and unpredictable (pp. 192-193).

Collaboration, like time, can be a subject for struggle between administrators and teachers. The very nature of collaboration as an unpredictable, teacher-led process encourages some administrators to erect the safe simulation of contrived collegiality that can be more controlled than the reality of collaboration. Gardner (1999a) suggests that while we must all become comfortable with change, we must also remain conscious of the constants in human experiences. The challenges before educators are staggering, but the alternative to facing the challenges is unacceptable. All effective educators believe in a better future, for that is the essence of our business. Figuring out the best path to take for schools to accommodate what the past and present have given us, and to then plan for a brighter future, is the greatest challenge and opportunity any professional can face. Given the fact that education is concerned with our children and their future, the stakes become astronomical. The following sections, "Thinking," "Social Learning," and "Constructivism," were crafted to shed some light on areas of teaching and learning that relate to the challenges of educators in general and to collaboration in the schools in particular. Many overlapping themes will be discussed, but each area of discussion has its own abundant body of literature.

THINKING

John-Steiner (1997) explores thinking and creativity in her book *Notebooks of the Mind: Explorations of Thinking*. She divides thinking into visual, verbal, and scientific, and yet certain aspects of each, like the power of imagery, illustrate the difficulty in separating these areas of study. In exploring creativity, she looks at the externalization of thought. The substantial overlap in the divisions she created is evident since the creative acts she includes in her study involve many modalities of thought. Her focus, then, is on the transformations that characterize the externalization of thought. The nature of inner thought needs to be studied within the developmental, cognitive, and affective domains.

Educational researchers have been grappling with finding the best strategy to stimulate growth in student thinking. Because of the wide array of strategies offered by numerous credible scholars, the notion of "teaching thinking" and how to begin to change the classroom culture to accommodate this innovation overwhelmed teachers. In 1988, the Association for Supervision and Curriculum Development (ASCD) published *Dimensions of Thinking: A Framework for Curriculum and Instruction* (Marzano et al.) in an attempt to clarify thinking instruction. They identified over thirty programs or approaches designed for teaching thinking. Each program included a definition of thinking and various options for instruction. What they found to be missing was an organizing framework that gave educators some structure for thought, a common knowledge base, and a common language for teaching thinking. The authors drew from many scholarly works to identify five dimensions of thinking that run through both research and theory: metacognition, critical and creative thinking, thinking processes, core thinking skills, and the relationship of content-area knowledge to thinking. Their major concern in producing this framework based on the five dimensions of thinking is that educators will use it in isolation. Instead, they hope that educators will develop in all students a healthy knowledge base and provide students with cognitive and metacognitive tools and strategies that will enable them to use the knowledge effectively in meaningful contexts.

Halpern (1996) defines *metacognition* as "what we know about what we know" (p. 28). She finds that most people are unaware of the nature of their own thinking processes or even the existence of thinking processes that lead to their judgments and conclusions about matters. Mental management, a broader term that encompasses metacognition, features prominently in several recent studies of thinking. In *The Thinking Classroom: Learning and Teaching in a Culture of Thinking,* Tishman, Perkins, and Jay (1995) suggest that a classroom culture of thinking in which the environment has a number of forces in it which work together to foster good thinking is our best strategy to improve student thinking.

"I Tried This"

The development of a learning community in a school—one that fosters collaboration and experimentation—is not trivial or easy, but it clearly is essential. So, too, is the culture of failure and of being able to stand up and say, "I tried this and it did not work well, but here is what I learned and what I will do differently next time."–*Teacher Educator*

Mental management is concerned both with students' metacognition and how the classroom culture can encourage students to take control of their thinking creatively and effectively. Sternberg (1997) sets out a schema of mental self-management in *Thinking Styles* that has undertones of metacognition running throughout each form of government. In *Intelligence Reframed: Multiple Intelligences for the 21st Century,* Gardner (1999b) contends that thinking varies across domains, although certain habits of thought are universally useful. These habits of mind, such as brainstorming, taking one's time, eliciting feedback, and putting work aside when a snag appears, are weak and must be practiced within every domain to be useful.

In *Teachers as Cultural Workers: Letters to Those Who Dare Teach*, Freire (1998) rails against prepackaged teachers' materials because an authoritarian outside source dictates what will be taught in the teachers' classrooms and strips teachers of both the control and the need to think creatively. Freire claims that "what is ironic in all of this is that sometimes these experts, who overload their teaching packages with detail, even explicitly promote their materials by stating that one of the main objectives of their teaching packages (though they don't call their materials 'packages') is to train prospective teachers to become critical, daring, and creative" (p. 8). Freire finds it shocking that the teachers who become subservient to the packages are then limited in their own creativity and "are restrained from producing what the prepackaged practice promises: children who enjoy freedom, who are critical and creative" (p. 9).

In conversations with Jean-Claude Bringuier (1977/1980), Jean Piaget explained that "education, for most people, means trying to lead the child to resemble the typical adult of his society. . . . But for me, education means making creators, even if there aren't many of them, even if the creations of one are limited by comparison with those of another. But you have to make inventors, innovators, not conformists" (p. 132).

SOCIAL LEARNING

Piaget's psychology can be compared and contrasted with Bruner's (Wood, 1988). Piaget was interested in the structure of thought whereas Bruner described processes that are present in problem solving. They both place emphasis on action and problem solving in learning. Bruner's psychology tended to consider language, communication, and instruction as important in the development of knowledge and understanding. Piaget acknowledges social interaction and communication as having a role in his theory, but it plays a less important part in the development of intelligence than in Bruner's view. In that sense, Bruner can be viewed as having more in common with Vygotsky, who placed instruction at the center of human development.

In *Mind in Society: The Development of Higher Psychological Processes*, Vygotsky (1978) claimed that "learning is not development but properly organized learning results in mental development and sets into motion a variety of developmental processes that would be impossible apart from learning. Thus, learning is a necessary and universal aspect of the process of developing culturally organized, specifically human, psychological functions" (p. 90). Vygotsky held that developmental processes lagged behind the learning process, and that sequence resulted in zones of proximal development which are defined as "the distance between the child's actual developmental level as determined by independent problem solving and the level of potential development as determined through problem solving under adult guidance or in collaboration with more capable peers" (p. 86). His hypothesis established the unity of learning processes and internal developmental processes.

In *Everyday Cognition: Its Development in Social Context,* Rogoff and Lave (1984) agree that interaction with other people and uses of socially provided tools are central to the everyday contexts in which cognitive activity occurs. "People, usually in conjunction with each other and always guided by social norms, set goals, negotiate appropriate means to reach the goals, and assist each other in implementing the means and resetting the goals as activities evolve" (p. 4). Following Vygotsky's theory, they claim that the social system in which the child is embedded channels cognitive development. In their view, the development of the child is guided by social interaction to adapt to the intellectual tools and skills of the culture.

Rogoff (1990) elaborates on this Vygotsky-inspired view in *Apprenticeship in Thinking: Cognitive Development in Social Contexts* by identifying two levels of sociocultural phenomena: apprenticeship, which involves social interaction carried out by adult-child and child-child dyads in problem-solving contexts; and guided participation, which assumes that both guidance and participation in culturally valued activities are essential to children's apprenticeship in thinking. Rogoff also discusses intersubjectivity as the shared understanding based on a common focus of attention and shared presuppositions that form the ground for communication.

Vygotsky viewed learning as a profoundly social process that emphasized dialogue and different roles that language, signs, and symbols play in instruction and in mediated cognitive growth. Several followers of Vygotsky's psychology focus on the peer collaboration aspect of his theory (Tudge, 1990; Brown & Campione, 1994; Wertsch & Toma, 1995). The first successful application of a prominent role for social contexts in the classroom experience was in the guise of the cooperative learning strategy.

> **Grow and Evolve**
>
> Communities grow and evolve, and are also inclusive, but sometimes communities become difficult to enter because they have their own languages and customs.
> —*Teacher Educator*

Learning strategies that encourage student interactions including peer collaboration while learning have become common since the late 1980s. A standard guide in support of this socially situated learning theory, Slavin's (1990) *Cooperative Learning: Theory, Research, and Practice* is

immensely popular with teachers. In Slavin's cooperative groups, students have specific roles and tasks. Teachers can gingerly modify their lesson plans to include group work while retaining much of the control over the groups. Group projects are now commonplace in the classroom from kindergarten through twelfth grade. While teachers have used different forms of cooperative learning methods for many years, it is a recent development that these methods have become pervasive at every grade and in every subject.

Brown and Campione's (1992) work with "Students as Researchers and Teachers" led to the community of learners aspect of the collaborative learning classroom. They argue that "asking students to form a research community in which they are responsible for their own and others' learning encouraged them to feel a sense of ownership for the knowledge they were acquiring" (p. 56). Using the reading group as their example, Brown and Campione contrast the community of learners with traditional practices. In the traditional group the teacher assigns the text, knows all the answers, and is the primary consumer of written products. In the community of learners, students read in order to write texts and work at their own pace; students read in order to understand, communicate, teach, write, and persuade. Students answer their own questions. "Teaching is on a need to know basis, with experts (be they children or adults) acting as facilitators" (p. 57). In McGilly's *Classroom Lessons: Integrating Cognitive Theory*, Brown and Campione (1994) describe their work by comparing it to Dewey's "discovery learning" concept from his pedagogical creed (1897/1972).

Brown and Campione are wary of unguided discovery and are equally cautious about stepping into didactic instruction territory. They argue for a middle ground between didactic teaching and unguided discovery learning that they call "guided discovery" (p. 230). In guided discovery in a community of learners (GDCL), the teacher models, fosters, and guides the discovery process into forms of disciplined inquiry that may not have been reached without expert guidance. Karpov and Haywood (1998) recognize GDCL as an example of putting Vygotsky's idea of metacognitive mediation into classroom practice.

In their communities of learners, Brown and Campione view the classroom as comprised of multiple zones of proximal development through which the students learn to navigate via different routes and at different rates. In GDCL, a zone can include adults, children, and resources such as books, videos, the Internet, and computer databases. Their definition of a zone is that it "embodies a concept of readiness to learn that emphasizes upper, rather than lower, levels of competence, boundaries that are not immutable, but rather constantly changing as the learner becomes increasingly independent at successively more advanced levels" (p. 236). To those who are familiar with optimal experience

Different Points of View

One of the most impressive models of collaboration in education is reflected in the work of educators in Reggio Emilia, northern Italy. The Italians put a lovely twist on the concept of collaboration-the importance and need for disagreements in collaborative relationships! They expect, invite, and thrive on differences in point of view, and they say there is no point in working together with one another as educators if they think alike and have no differences.

—Teacher Educator

as defined by Csikszentmihalyi's (1990) theory of flow, guided discovery in a community of learners sounds like the analogous equivalent of flow enhancing the quality of classroom life. Brown (1997) described her research known as Fostering Communities of Learners in "Transforming Schools into Communities of Thinking and Learning about Serious Matters." She describes a visit from Bruner, who singled out four ideas underlying fostering communities of learners: agency, or controlling your own mental activity; reflection, taking time to understand what you learn; collaboration, "sharing the resources of the mix of human beings involved in teaching and learning" (p. 399); and culture, the way of life and thought in the classroom. In *The Culture of Education,* Bruner (1996) calls Brown a leading figure in the intimate nature of teaching and school learning

The National Study of School Evaluation (NSSE) published *Indicators of Schools of Quality: A Research-Based Self-Assessment Guide for Schools Committed to Continuous Improvement* in 1997 (Fitzpatrick). The mission of this study was to "develop state-of-the-art evaluation materials and services to enhance and promote student growth and school improvement" (p. vi). NSSE published this study to help focus attention on the factors that have proven to make a difference in improving student learning. In "Part 2: Focusing on the Quality of the Work of the School, Section 2: Quality Organizational Systems: Community-Building, Principle 9," it is stated that community-building conditions and working relationships are fostered within the school. Ten indicators under the subheading "The school fosters collaborative and interdependent teams to achieve goals" are included under Principle 9. Principle 10 states that "The school community is expanded and strengthened through collaborative networks of support for student learning" (p. 178).

CONSTRUCTIVISM

In *Creating and Sustaining the Constructivist Classroom,* Marlowe and Page (1998) define the main proposition of constructivism as learning, constructing, creating, inventing, and developing one's own knowledge. Learning, in constructivist terms, is both a process and a result of questioning, interpreting, and analyzing information; using information and thinking processes to build and alter our meaning and understanding of

concepts and ideas; and integrating current experiences with our past experiences. The focus in constructivism is on thinking, understanding, and applying as opposed to the traditional approach of accumulating, memorizing, and reciting. Traditional methods are advantageous in terms of administrative management since they are time-efficient, orderly, and predictable.

Exploring what we know about our educational system, Brooks and Brooks (1993) examined five factors about the classroom. In *In Search of Understanding: The Case for Constructivist Classrooms,* they describe the traditional orientation as the domination by teacher talk, heavy reliance on textbooks, growing interest in cooperative learning, a devaluation of student thinking, and the premise that there exists a fixed world that the learner must come to know. Conversely, they see the goals of the constructivist orientation as teachers wanting students to take responsibility for their own learning, to be autonomous thinkers, to develop integrated understandings of concepts, and to pose and seek the answers to important questions. The difference in regard to the static, passive nature of the traditional teacher-centered classroom as compared to the dynamic, active nature of the constructivist learner-centered classroom is fairly obvious to observers. The constructivist classroom addresses the student lament of boredom and disengagement (Steinberg, 1996).

The engagement that students feel from the social dimension to learning (both collaborative and cooperative learning) is energizing and leads to deeper understanding. Constructivist teaching practices that encourage such engagement generally take more time and put teachers under more pressure to cover the content in the curriculum. In "The Many Faces of Constructivism," Perkins (1999) says that strict constructivists "argue that process is all while others believe that students need to arrive at an understanding of the best theories propounded by the disciplines" (p. 8). In the worst-case scenario, constructivist practices can seem manipulative when there is a best or a right way to be discovered. Perkins describes three learner roles in constructivism: the active learner, who discusses, debates, investigates, and hypothesizes; the social learner, who understands that knowledge and understanding are co-constructed in dialogue with others; and the creative learner, who creates or re-creates knowledge. Perkins suggests that constructivism enjoys strong advocacy in part because psychological research shows that active engagement in learning may lead to better retention, understanding, and active use of knowledge. Fogarty (1999), in "Architects of

Know What You Know

Know what you know and what you don't know—recognize your own strengths and weaknesses. Recognize the expertise of the other person, his/her willingness to share, engage in give and take—different perspectives.—*Administrator*

the Intellect," identifies Dewey, Piaget, Vygotsky, Feuerstein, Gardner, and Diamond as leading proponents of a constructivist theory. They "speak elegantly to the creative genius of the teacher as architect" (p. 76). Fogarty distills their contributions into seven elements that define the constructivist philosophy: "learner- and life-centered curriculum enriched environments; interactive settings; differentiated instruction; inquiry, experimentation, and investigation; mediation and facilitation; and metacognitive reflection" (p. 78).

In "How Compatible Are Radical Constructivism, Sociocultural Approaches, and Social Constructivism?" Confrey (1995) predicts an alternative theory to Vygotsky and Piaget that will establish a distinct basis in which diversity plays a more significant role and "in which the individuality of the child is tempered by the responsibility of community and culture" (p. 225). Confrey claims that we need to recognize that individual and social development shape each other and seek an appropriate balance of each. Confrey views experience and context as intermingled. In "Leading the Conversations," Lambert (1995) signifies conversations as the medium for the reciprocal processes that "enable participants in a school community to construct meanings toward a common purpose about teaching and learning" (p. 83).

Lambert defines the primary role of the constructivist leader as the one who leads the conversations. Conversations, in Lambert's terms, that are constructivist in nature are characterized by "shared intention of 'truth-seeking,' remembrances and reflections of the past, a search for meaning in the present, a mutual revelation of ideas and information, and respectful listening" (p. 85). Conversations, of course, may not include all of the elements during each interaction, but all the elements are implied or understood based on prior experiences with the relationships of the conversationalists. The conversations occur within the context of a trusting environment. Lambert contends that leading conversations is a shared responsibility and a skilled undertaking for which each participant needs to be prepared.

> **What You Bring to the Table**
>
> What you bring to the table is who you are as a professional–collaboration calls forth your expertise to blend and meld it with the ideas of others.–*Administrator*

Brooks and Brooks (1999) identify two main criticisms of constructivism as an educational approach. In "The Courage to Be Constructivist," they discuss the critique that suggests that constructivism is too permissive (i.e., constructivist teachers follow the whims of their students without concern for the curriculum). The other critique is that constructivist approaches to education lack rigor. Brooks and Brooks contend

that state and local curriculums address *what* students learn, and constructivism addresses *how* students learn. The goal of the constructivist teacher is to "blend the *what* with the *how*" (p. 23).

Henderson (1996) suggests that we imagine a nation whose citizens were educated at schools that function in a constructivist manner as centers of inquiry. "How comfortable would they be with subject matter inquiry, personal inquiry, and social inquiry? Who would be their heroes and heroines? What kind of society would they support? What would be their politics?" (p. 218). Acknowledging that it may be some time before most teachers find their ways to schools that function as centers of inquiry, he challenges teachers to imagine themselves as potential transformative teacher-leaders and to carry that vision with them wherever they are teaching. Transformative teachers reflect upon their practice and strive to improve in a variety of ways. The next chapter introduces us to the recent history of teacher research and the profound changes that are occurring both in teacher/action research and professional development. The role of action research in education in America needs to be acknowledged, and educators who seek to be transformative in their schools should take heed.

CHAPTER 5

The Professional Community

NEW SCHOLARSHIP

Anderson and Herr (1999) contend that the struggle for new scholarship belongs to both the academics and the practitioners and that together they will define what accounts for practitioner research. Presenting an academic perspective, they cite a university professor who bemoans the abundance of practicality that teachers have and recommend reading Tolstoy and other authors from the Western canon. Many school districts that seem to view practitioner research in a positive light are not so hung up on the specifics of "research" but are in a hurry to formalize it as a method of professional development. Anderson and Herr sound rather skeptical about the institutionalization of practitioner research. They argue that if it becomes institutionalized, it will dull the critical power of the movement and have little effect on bringing about real change in educational practices.

Morocco and Solomon (1999) recognize the need to reinvent a new model of professional development that joins staff developers and teachers together to build a common professional community. They hold that the boundaries become blurred as teachers seek advanced research courses and become responsible for facilitating professional growth in their schools. Morocco and Solomon discuss "trainer of trainer" institutes "that build a body of colleagues who can provide ongoing support to one another and ongoing connections to mentors as they learn to facilitate a curriculum design process" (pp. 248-249). They contend that the blurring of the boundaries should be intentional and see the goal as a distribution of expertise over time, among all the professionals in the community. Thereby, a teacher's development from novice to expert would be seen as a natural evolution.

The melding of professional development into the natural teacher development cycle sounds like an idea whose time has come. The standards movement notwithstanding, it promotes the notion that teachers are responsible for not only their classrooms but for their schools. It provides an environment in which a school learning community encompasses all the professionals in the building, students, parents, and community. In fact, the standards movement can be viewed as a catalyst to pursue a teacher research program that investigates the best methods of accommodating state and national standards along with the school and district mission statements. While everything might look rosy from this vantage point, it is necessary to highlight some obstacles to teacher research.

TEACHER/ACTION/INSIDER/PRACTITIONER RESEARCH

The preservice educator who learns that inquiry is an integral part of her future as an effective teacher who strives to improve instruction will be equipped with the skills and tools of the action researcher. Practitioner inquiry, practitioner research, action research, teacher research, insider research, and teacher inquiry are all defined by educators' deliberate, systematic inquiry into ongoing instructional situations. The greatest challenge to the preservice educator described above is the standards movement that removes the agenda regarding curriculum, assessment, and instruction from the school. In "The Teacher Research Movement: A Decade Later," Cochran-Smith and Lytle (1999) write that the impact of the standards movement de-emphasizes the local school context, construction of local knowledge, and the teacher's role as an active participant in school change. Certainly Cochran-Smith and Lytle's outlook for the future of teacher research is bleak.

THE "HOW-TO" OF TEACHER RESEARCH

In *Inside/Outside: Teacher Research and Knowledge*, Cochran-Smith and Lytle (1993) identify four major obstacles to teacher research. First, they consider teacher isolation as described by Lortie (1975) and Goodlad (1984) as a fundamental problem. They view teacher research as a collaborative and social activity that requires opportunities for shared intellectual experiences. As Lortie and Goodlad reported, the school day leaves little time for teachers to collaborate. Second, school cultures (occupational socialization) discourage teachers from discussing their failures and problems, and yet that is the language of teacher research. Teacher researchers need to ask uncomfortable, probing questions regarding areas that are possible targets for improvement. Third, the issue about the knowledge base for teaching is unsettled. The technical view of teaching constructed by university researchers is the norm while the teacher researcher movement is based on the premise that professionals play participatory roles in the creation and use of their knowledge base. And fourth, they, "somewhat ironically," point to the poor reputation of educational research among teachers. Research has done nothing but point out deficits in teaching, and researchers have never learned to approach teachers in an understandable way. "The fact that most educational research is perceived by teachers as irrelevant to their daily lives spills into and contaminates their willingness to believe both that teacher research has the potential to be relevant and that they themselves might want to be researchers" (1993, p. 89).

Within the body of literature pertaining to teacher research, there are a number of "how-to" books that offer guides to the process. Following Waller's (1932) observations about teachers and their propensity for "shop talk," teacher research has a natural point of departure. In *The Art of Classroom Inquiry: A Handbook for Teacher-Researchers,* Hubbard and Power (1993) talk about how teachers meet in faculty lounges, hallways, conferences, and college classrooms to share stories, frustrations, and triumphs.

Voices

Do not make concessions to the but-we-don't-have-time voices. Of course collaboration takes time. That is why community is so important. Establishing a functional relationship and describing a shared vision take a lot of time.–*Practitioner*

Budding teacher researchers develop professionally by using their peers and students as collaborators and their classrooms and schools as laboratories. Calling teacher researchers "a wonderful new breed of artists-in-residence" (p. xiii), Hubbard and Power take teachers through the stages of research, from finding and framing a research question to collecting data, designing research, analyzing data, reviewing the literature, and writing up the research. They emphasize the importance of networking with other teacher researchers throughout the research process.

In their chapter, "Lives of Inquiry: Communities of Learning and Caring," Tafel and Fischer in *Teachers Doing Research: Practical Possibilities* (Burnaford et al., 1996) discuss sustaining the relationship between teacher research and professional development. They identify four recurring themes: (1) caring relationships and dialogue with colleagues; (2) teacher ownership of their teaching, decisions, and responsibility to the communities of learning and inquiry must be an essential feature; (3) constructing knowledge through reflections on practice is a main goal; and (4) the kinds of questions that teachers pursue are based on personal values and beliefs that guide their teaching and learning (pp. 134-135).

In his contribution to the "how-to" of teacher research, Glanz (1998) starts by confronting the "bad rap" given to research. In discussing the marginal role research plays in schools today, Glanz argues that the inclination to avoid research is "shortsighted, provincial, and possibly deleterious" (p. 1). He goes through the same steps that Hubbard and Power (1993, pp. 233-239) present and adds seven suggestions for action researchers:

1. Expect the unexpected.
2. Be receptive to both quantitative and especially qualitative approaches.
3. Give it your all.
4. Don't make a decision too quickly.
5. Keep lines of communication open and clear.
6. Yes, appreciate your enlightened eye.
7. Take action (p. 239).

Glanz describes educational leaders as thoughtful, reflective practitioners who are committed to inquiry and scholarship.

COMMUNITIES OF SCHOLAR-TEACHERS

In *Reflective Teaching: The Study of Your Constructivist Practices,* Henderson (1996) invites the teacher to become a career-long student of one's own teaching. He reiterates what many who write about teacher research as professional development stress: that the school is a center of inquiry. Henderson places this view in the context of constructivist teaching practices that can be defined as "any deliberate, thoughtful educational activity that is designed to facilitate students' active understanding" (p. 6). Reflective constructivist practices and teacher inquiry are recognized as essential elements in teacher research.

> **Engage with Others**
>
> According to Vygotsky, "Intelligence is the capacity to make use of the help of others." This is a revolutionary idea—that what is important about the mind is not what any of us knows but how we use what we know to engage with others around us in a huge variety of ways.—*Teacher Educator*

The process of teacher research is often described as cyclical in nature. After group reflection on action taken (based on teacher research), a group decision is made to either continue or to modify the "results" (Noffke & Stevenson, 1995; Glanz, 1998). This continuous cycle raises the question of evaluation of teacher research. In their review,

"The Teacher Research Movement: A Decade Later," Cochran-Smith and Lytle (1999) discuss "The Methods Critique" of the teacher research movement. They claim that some education researchers question whether teacher research is research at all. The researchers question the research using traditional criteria for qualitative research.

Just as Lincoln and Guba (1985) identify special criteria for trustworthiness of naturalistic inquiry, Anderson and Herr (1999) suggest "redefining rigor" (p. 16) for insider research. They address issues of "validity" that might help to legitimate practitioner research and/or help to define the boundaries of such research. Anderson and Herr describe five types of validity: outcome validity, where actions lead to resolution of the problem; process validity, where the framing of the problems leads to ongoing learning; democratic validity, where the research is done in collaboration with all the stakeholders; catalytic validity, where the likelihood of reorienting perceptions of reality in order to effect change exist; and dialogic validity, where the research is evaluated through a form of peer review. They suggest that "in order to promote both democratic and dialogic validity, some have insisted that practitioner research should only be done as collaborative inquiry" (p. 16). When the dialogic validity is stressed, these studies can achieve "goodness-of-fit" (p. 16) with the teacher community, both with respect to defining problems and in describing findings related to the research effort.

In *Teachers: The Missing Voice in Education*, Cohn and Kottkamp (1993) envision schools as communities of scholar-teachers where everyone collaborates on action research projects that have the capacity to change the structure of the school or significant elements within them. Once again, the school is seen as the center of inquiry. In order to restructure schools to accommodate this view, there are necessary changes in school conditions, including reducing teacher loads, encouraging collaboration over isolation, seeking out school-university partnerships, and providing an environment where teachers are protected from unreasonable time and accountability constraints.

Interdisciplinary Projects

Including a strong component on collaborative learning in an education course and practicing the model within other courses in a teacher preparation program are great interdisciplinary projects. Teachers should be prepared to work more effectively with colleagues not only within our departments but also within interdisciplinary projects. A strong theory base as well as guidelines for the process would be something for teachers to teach students.

—*Administrator*

Acquainting ourselves with the literature as we have thus far, we can surmise that collaboration in schools is recognized as a fundamental element of teacher research, professional development, and school reform efforts. Beyond collaborating with other teachers, teachers are encouraged to collaborate with resource educators, administrators, students, university professors, preservice educators, and parents. Societal influences on education and new social realities that impact classroom teaching shed light on the necessity for schools and communities to become partners in facing the challenges of educating our students in the new millennium.

PROFESSIONAL DEVELOPMENT

Transformative teachers have an understanding of staff development that is different than the traditional workshop led by an outside consultant. They are committed to collaborative study that generates new professional knowledge and supports teaching as a reflective practice. They have a strong commitment to making organizational learning a way of life (Senge, 1990). To these teachers, the developmental focus of staff development is on teachers' questions in a particular school community. They believe that teachers can act as catalysts for each other's learning and professional growth. In her article "Practices That Support Teacher Development," Lieberman (1995) highlights three points in describing a new approach to continuing professional development. First, staff development must exist in a culture of inquiry where professional learning is expected and an ongoing part of teaching and school life in general. Second, teachers should be decision makers in the substance and the process of staff development. Third, staff development activities should not be single, onetime events but part of a process of long-term professional study.

Staff development, professional development, and teacher development are synonyms for the continuing education of practitioners. There are a variety of vehicles for this information, including in-services, workshops, and conferences. Staff development and successful innovation or school improvements have often been linked together. In "Staff Development, Innovation, and Institutional Development," Fullan (1990) argues that although effective staff development can be identified, it is not often practiced. It is common for staff development to be a pawn in a political power play between administrators or between administrators and teachers. The central paradox of staff development is that while it is generally viewed as an essential strategy for school improvement, it often takes teachers away from their classes, and the community views that as a detriment to the quality of instruction at the school.

In an effort to join forces and share in the challenge of delivering effective staff development, some districts formed collaborative organizations as a cost-effective way to provide staff development and to promote the exchange of ideas (Taylor, Thompson, & Schmuck, 1989). Fullan

(1990) claims that the link between staff development and school achievement is fairly recent. He reports that studies conducted in the late 1970s and 1980s found significant results that demonstrate that carefully designed staff development strategies and effective implementation of innovations were positively interrelated. Fullan reports that "staff development should be innovation-related, continuous during the course of implementation, and involve a variety of formal (e.g., workshops) and informal (e.g., teacher-exchange) components" (p. 4). Job-embedded learning, professional development schools (PDSs), and Building Resource Teachers (BRTs) are a few prime examples of the wave of the future for staff development delivery.

JOB-EMBEDDED LEARNING

In contrast to the "sit and get" form of staff development (where specialists visit schools to provide staff development to teachers, who "sit and get" the information), job-embedded learning connects teacher learning with the immediate problems faced in the school. In *A New Vision for Staff Development,* Sparks and Hirsh (1997) claim that job-embedded learning is "based on the assumption that the most powerful learning is that which occurs in response to challenges currently being faced by the learner and that allows for immediate application, experimentation, and adaptation on the job" (p. 52). They argue that results-driven education, systems thinking, and constructivism are the three major educational ideas that impact staff development. The creation of constructivist classrooms requires staff development that is not the traditional, transmittal form but must model constructivist practices.

Clandinin and Connelly (1996) highlight the difficulty of anyone (including the professional development specialist) but the classroom teacher learning the "secret" (p. 25) story about what goes on inside the classroom. Sparks and Hirsh (1997) predict that the amount of formalized, off-site staff development will diminish in the future, and teachers and administrators will spend their professional development time learning in various forms of job-embedded activities. Job-embedded activities lend themselves to teacher inquiry groups, peer observation, collaborative lesson planning, and journal writing. These activities are most effective when teachers are familiar with reflective teaching practices.

FROM PDS TO BRT

The joint effort between teacher education programs and local school districts led to the development of professional development schools (PDSs). In *The Right to Learn: A Blueprint for Creating Schools That Work,* Darling-Hammond (1997) compares the PDS to a teaching hospital in the medical profession. The success of the PDS lies in the effective collaborative relationship between the university teacher education program and the school district. The schools are laboratories for state-of-the-art practice and are organized to teach new professionals and veteran teachers. The learning occurs for both the new teachers and for the senior teachers, who report that "they deepen their knowledge by serving as mentors, adjunct faculty, co-researchers, and teacher leaders" (p. 321). The real magic of the PDS program is that it seems to link theory and practice in education, a feat akin to pulling a rabbit out of a hat. Even teachers who have positive relationships with university faculty through PDS programs continue to have disdain for "theory talk" versus classroom verity (Hobbs et al., 1998).

The Building Resource Teacher (BRT) is a teacher who has release time from most teaching duties and who works with other teachers as a mentor, coach, and resource provider. Hayes, Grippe, and Hall (1999) report that BRTs "provide observation and feedback sessions, teach demonstration lessons, procure staff development resources, and give teachers at each school access to expert knowledge on teaching practice" (p. 18). They also collaborate with administrators, parents, and support personnel and act as a liaison between the school, district office, and community. The schools that have BRTs report that new teachers benefit from the on-site support, and veteran teachers and administrators find the BRTs accessible, in tune with the local needs, and effective at providing ongoing support. The districts that have BRT programs provide the teachers who become BRTs with their own ongoing support programs through the school district and related professional development experiences.

There Must Be a Plan

Unless all elements of a school building (teachers, support staff, and administrators) work together, collaboration will not move forward in a sufficient manner. In other words, there must be a plan that involves all parties to work toward establishing a community.—*Administrator*

The changes that teachers need to accommodate in their profession naturally impact the needs that they have for ongoing professional development. Lieberman and Miller (in Brandt, 2000) identify seven transitions that teachers have to make to realign themselves with the "new social realities of teaching" (p. 51). The transitions are in response to major shifts in perspective and practice:

⇒ *From individualism to professional community*—this requires a school culture that values collegiality and trust over autonomy and territoriality.

⇒ *From teaching at the center to learning at the center*—this requires the teacher to view the construction of learning at the heart of education and see learning as something that goes beyond the classroom.

⇒ *From technical work to inquiry*—this requires teachers to see themselves as reflective teachers who are engaged in the process of discovery along with their students.

⇒ *From control to accountability*—this requires teachers to focus on the public responsibility for student performance while recognizing the realities of the lives their students lead outside the classroom.

⇒ *From managed work to leadership*—this requires teachers to see themselves in a management role, as they become leaders in curriculum and instruction.

⇒ *From classroom concerns to whole school concerns*—this requires teachers to view the school as their workplace and not just the classroom. Teachers feel themselves to be members of active professional communities of learners.

⇒ *From a weak knowledge base to a stronger, broader one*—this presumes that research in human cognition and intelligence has helped teachers' efforts to professionalize their work (p. 51).

It is clear that the new social realities of teaching present a challenge for teacher learning, both in teacher education programs and professional development programs. The trend in professional development is toward local programs that benefit teachers in their daily practice. Within this new concept of local control of professional development, teacher inquiry or teacher research is viewed as professional staff development. In "Teacher Inquiry as Professional Staff Development," Richardson (1994) defines teacher inquiry as "an individual or group of teachers being systematically thoughtful about their teaching, students, and/or contexts" (p. 186).

Comfort Level

Unless participants understand the process and feel that they have the amount of time that is necessary, it will not work. It is not necessarily that they need more time but, rather, that they feel comfortable about working in a collaborative manner.—*Administrator*

The dilemma facing professional development is that the success of teacher inquiry is its dependence on primarily voluntary participation by teachers who develop their own agendas and courses of action.

Professional development has traditionally been controlled outside of the school at the district or state level. Richardson asks, "Can a school district promote and support teacher inquiry as staff development without sacrificing the essential elements and desirable effects of a process that has been undertaken spontaneously and voluntarily?" (p. 186).

Of the different types of staff development that facilitate teacher inquiry, Richardson identifies the collaborative process as the most useful. In this scenario, an outside facilitator guides the teacher inquiry process but does not overlay a top-down philosophy. The facilitator has deep content knowledge to share at appropriate times, is skilled in inquiry processes so that he or she can help teachers in their quest, and is sincerely interested in the topics under discussion. The important balance to maintain in this collaborative process is the power relationships among the participating teachers, administrators, and facilitators.

In her article about sustaining educational change, Moffett (2000) recognizes the critical role that professional development plays in the beginning and implementation phases of reform initiatives. She cites research that shows that education innovations thrive or fail by the amount and quality of assistance that their teachers get once the innovation is under way. The overload of innovations, policies, and initiatives coming at teachers from the school district and state education departments, including standards and achievement test protocols, presents a challenge to policymakers, administrators, and teachers. The ownership that teachers can have over their own learning processes should be one area that the powers that be should be able to piece together in the puzzle of sustaining educational change.

School Culture

Intangibles of school culture, and more overt things like whether teachers' efforts are acknowledged, whether the difficulty of change is understood, whether they are given time to try new things, etc., are important. That is a pretty tough challenge—to change school culture.–*Policymaker*

Teachers want to know that, at the end of the day, the art of teaching counts as much as the science and management. In their hearts and minds, they work for their students and not their districts. Working together as professionals makes the journey healthier and richer and deeper.

What thinking skills do educators need to pursue investigation in the classroom? Ways of thinking about teaching, learning, and thinking that are fundamental to educator collaboration are discussed in the next chapter, "A Collaborative Mind-Set."

PART **II** SET

CHAPTER **6**

A Collaborative Mind-Set

Collaborative partners have characteristics that lend themselves to succeed in a collegial environment in the school. This is not to say that collaboration skills cannot be taught. The message of this book is that those skills can be identified and practiced by all educators. Nevertheless, there is a predominating *collaborative mind-set,* if you will, that allows for those elements identified as essential to exist and to thrive. The topics covered in this chapter acknowledge a few of those characteristics. This is not a comprehensive discourse on the subject. We are not looking out at other scholars' research so much as learning about ways of looking within ourselves as educators and learners. This chapter does, however, give you a few established vantage points from which to view the collaborative mind-set. The challenge before you is to take this information, reflect upon it, and begin to construct your own criteria of what is essential for true partnership in education.

The term *mind-set* is one that we use when discussing someone's frame of mind or point of view. In this chapter a mind-set is defined similarly as "perceptual frameworks shaped by and supported through experience, education, social conditioning, and language" (Thornton & McEntee, 1995, p. 250). Mind-sets exist in schools as they do in every other arena of society. Teachers, administrators, staff, and students have both individual and collective mind-sets. Viewing learning and knowing as co-constructed social processes begs the question of the mind-set of both groups of learners, the students and the educators. You will find that there is overlap in some of these areas, but the focal point will be unique. Some areas come to us directly from psychology, some are directly from education, and some are from educational psychology. Try them on and see how they fit. Do you find yourself as a learner described in any section more than any other? Does the overlap of topics help you to picture yourself trying on a new lens to see how it fits?

As a context for a collaborative mind-set, we are envisioning a learner-centered school environment. This is one where the process of learning and knowing is co-constructed and is shared by the educators and students who come together in a social context. This constructivist approach to education does not have to exist exclusively but can be intermixed with traditional approaches depending on the goals of the curricular unit. Similarly, educators who have a natural tendency to collaborate with colleagues make choices and are not solely dependent upon collaborative relationships for all of their curricular work.

We begin framing the mind-set with metacognition, which gives us a broad context within which we can place the other topics. Mindfulness and aspects of critical and creative thinking are important to bring to the table as valuable collaborative partners. Consider whether the concept of "habits of mind" is counterintuitive to mindfulness and whether it allows for sharing and dynamic collaborative thought processes. And lastly, let us think about our global goals and consider how social justice can fit into the collaborative mind-set. The opportunity in education to impact one's worldview is not only for our students, it is for us educators as well.

METACOGNITION

"So I thought to myself, Self, I thought . . ." Perhaps you have not spoken these very words, but you might say something along the lines of "I need time to think about that." If you are of a certain age you may even remember tying a "thinking cap" under your chin. The cap actually predated the research on metacognition that grew in popularity over the last twenty years. This concept covers more than thinking about thinking. It also includes the self-regulation of how we go about learning. The key to metacognition is self-awareness of our individual cognitive or thinking and learning systems.

It seems logical that having more knowledge about our own thinking and learning strategies will help us as we work together with others in a collaborative partnership. Making our thought processes explicit requires some metacognitive skills, and it is not uncommon for partners to share the genesis of an original idea.

The kinds of questions that we ask ourselves as metacognitive thinkers can range from *Did I understand what I read?* to *What is the best way for me to break down this problem/project?* Educators who concern themselves with their students' thinking processes are most likely versed in metacognitive skills. Collaborative partners who monitor their group's thought processes may have a type of "group think" started where the common language that is applied to the collaborative experience is also used to explain and regulate cognitive systems that are ongoing in the partnership.

Researchers in metacognition have found that these skills are not a part of our natural development as mature thinkers. Explicit instruction and metacognitive experiences are necessary to develop these skills in learners. Any collaborative partnership will benefit from discussions about thinking processes and, once again, will model this behavior for potential use with students.

Those strategies that teachers use in classrooms to allow for actual thinking are recommended for collaborative partnerships as well. Wait time is important for all of us whether we are adolescent or adult learners. Ask someone why she is suggesting something so that we can understand her comment more fully. Think aloud in your partnership so that together you can model both thinking about what you know and thinking about regulating or monitoring how you can go about learning more about your project.

If you were to study metacognition in depth you might find strong similarities to cognition and wonder about the distinction between the strategies for both. You want to identify the "known" and the "unknown" and define your task. And you will want to plan or regulate your learning. Metacognition is also concerned with explicitly thinking and talking about thinking and your learning processes. We need a thinking vocabulary, and we need to hear those words from role models who can show us explicitly how to think about thinking. Collaborative partnerships provide the perfect forum for practicing your metacognitive skills. You might find that you and/or your partnership decide to keep a journal documenting your thinking processes so that you can look back at it at any point in time for clarification or reflection. Debriefing, wrapping up, and closure methods are recommended as valuable metacognitive skills; they lead thinkers to learn about themselves as thinkers and at their progress over the course of a project. All of these skills and strategies help us to know ourselves better as learners and can only help us in enriching our roles as educators.

For one to be metacognitive, one must be mindful about one's own thinking and learning. Mindfulness has its own body of knowledge within the context of metacognition.

Choice

Choice is an essential component. Collaborative partners cannot be assigned from above; they have to be approached and solicited. For the level of motivation and creativity to be maintained, collaborative partners must be mutually chosen.–*Practitioner*

MINDFULNESS

To be mindful sounds like it means to be thoughtful. One distinction is that being thoughtful does not require conscious and fresh consideration. One may act in a thoughtful way by being very considerate or by

remembering an important event in someone else's life. These can be rote ways of behaving, albeit considerate.

Mindfulness refers more specifically to a consciousness of thought, an active awareness of how we are processing information and what we are doing with that new information once we have it. In her work on mindfulness, professor of psychology Ellen J. Langer (1990) of Harvard University identifies three qualities of a mindful state of being: (1) creation of new categories, (2) openness to new information, and (3) awareness of more than one perspective (p. 62).

Take these three categories and relate them to collaborative partnerships in education. If the connections cannot be made with examples from any of your collaborative experiences (in or outside of education), create scenarios that reflect these qualities of mind.

Creation of New Categories

Consider the benefits of collaborating with someone outside of your subject area or grade level. Those categories that you both use in a routine way will be ill equipped to contain your new collaborative ideas. Certainly you will each use what you know from your background to help define the categories, but together you will create new categories that become the common language of your collaborative community. This process is continuous as your collaborative efforts progress and evolve.

In *The Power of Mindful Learning,* Langer (1997) takes a broad view of the concept of learning, including schooling, job, and home. She defines the differences between intelligence and mindfulness. A distinction is made between intelligence, which "depends on remembered facts and learned skills in contexts that are sometimes perceived as novel," and mindfulness, which "depends on the fluidity of knowledge and skills and recognizes both advantages and disadvantages in each" (p. 110). Flexibility of thought is considered to be a quality of intelligent thinking. The difference lies in the constructs that are applied to new situations. In looking at intelligence we view constructs as fixed, and used flexibly they can apply to novel contexts. In mindfulness, the learner does not look to pre-existing constructs to create a solution but rather creates new options by creating new categories based on new information gleaned from various perspectives.

Openness to New Information

Being open to new information does not sound like a radical notion since educators are faced with new information at mind-boggling speed in the information age. There is a difference, however, in tolerating the reality of a constant stream of new information and welcoming it with receptivity and openness. The openness implies the readiness to create

new categories and to accept that those categories will need to be changed yet again as you receive yet newer information. As human beings, we are designed to receive new information. As educators, we are sometimes loath to receive information that we understand will necessitate a shifting of established thought processes and categories.

Mindfulness demands a level of openness that perhaps does not come as readily as we would like to think it would. The constant theme running through Langer's work on mindfulness is fluidity and the comfort the mindful learner has in always recognizing that this process is one of being open, stepping back, looking around, and regrouping. In order for educators to seek to teach our students to be mindful, we need to look inward first and try to discover who we are as learners.

Awareness of More than One Perspective

Again, as educators in this information age, we are aware that the content knowledge we once had mastery over is now more of a foundation than an entire body of knowledge. No longer can any student, educator, or scholar profess to have the single perspective on any one area of knowledge. Accepting this fact and having an active awareness of it are two different things. An awareness of more than one perspective as a quality of mindfulness implies a willingness to consider one's own perspective as just one among two, three, or more.

Each of these three characteristics of mindfulness relates to each of us as educators and as collaborative partners. Each can also be applied to our partnerships and the propensity that some have toward exclusiveness. Whereas a partnership of two or more educators has created a common language by creating new categories, the partners need to be mindful when relating to other partnerships and again be eager to create yet newer categories that contain those that were newly created and those from another partnership. Partnerships need to be receptive to yet newer information that may alter the course of their collaborative process. And, in opening up their partnership, educators must always be vigilant to welcome more than their own perspective even if it is a newly created joint perspective based on a collaborative process. The concept of mindfulness reflects on the ongoing, generative nature of the collaborative process in education.

> **Infectious Enthusiasm**
>
> The enthusiasm experienced by the teachers as a result of collaboration is infectious in the classroom. Teachers play on each other's strengths to build a unique and energetic learning environment.—*Practitioner*

Various perspectives may not just mean other perspectives on the same intellectual level as the educator's level. Consider the overwhelming data that recognize the critical importance of the educator's respect

for the student. From a mindful perspective, the "wrong" answer coming from a student is one of those various perspectives; experienced teachers might consider comments from novice teachers relating to their content area or grade level as a form of various perspectives (and vice versa, perhaps relating to instructional technology); misunderstandings or miscommunications between colleagues may be considered various perspectives. As educators we can think at a particular intellectual level, but the risk we take is that we might be missing various perspectives that would help us rethink the new information we are processing and the new categories we are continuously creating.

CRITICAL THINKING

It is unfortunate that "critical" thinking sounds so draconian. It could be called "directed thinking" because that is the essence of critical thinking. Basically, it is the process of thinking that uses thinking strategies and skills toward the most effective outcome. It is directed, purposeful, and very definitely goal-oriented. If the term *critical thinking* sounds redundant, consider undirected thinking processes like daydreaming or that twilight thinking just before you drift off to sleep. Those types of thinking have their own purposes, but that is not what we are talking about here. In fact, most modes of thinking, including understanding and application thinking, fall somewhere between these two ends of the spectrum.

The study of critical thinking has really exploded in the last twenty years. Cognitive psychologists concur that we can in fact teach thinking strategies and skills with very positive outcomes. Thinking styles have become as well known in educational psychology as learning styles. In her comprehensive text *Thought and Knowledge: An Introduction to Critical Thinking,* Diane F. Halpern (1996, third edition, pp. 30-32) shares a framework that covers all types of thinking, which will help us think about thinking:

- ❀ What is the goal?
- ❀ What is known?
- ❀ Which thinking skill or skills will get you to your goal?
- ❀ Have you reached your goal?

Critical thinking requires clarity of *goals.* This is not to say that the goals cannot change. In terms of a collaborative partnership, it is imperative that all players are on the same page with the goals at all times. Collaboration and critical thinking are both goal-directed. Clear goals help the thinking process, and it helps to establish a path for the collaborative partners. Real-life goals can be messy and unfocused, but the act

of breaking them down into manageable, directed, purposeful goals for thinking helps bring the task into focus.

Deciding *what is known* is an important step in the foundation of the critical thinking process. Collaborative partners may have different views of what is known (which adds to the richness of the collaboration), and a consensus may need to be reached. The "knowns" or the "givens" are critical pieces of the puzzle. They may be returned to at any time, and some knowns may prove to be more important than others throughout the collaborative process.

Following the framework established above, we now know our goals, where we are going, and our knowns, where we are now. The power of critical thinking resides in choosing the most effective *thinking skills* to increase the probability of a desirable outcome. For a full understanding of critical thinking strategies and skills, see the work of Richard Paul and also Diane F. Halpern. To consider your own strategies think about the steps you take to plan an involved vacation or to compare prices when you are buying a car. How do you go about making daily decisions? In a conversation, how do you analyze the speaker's argument and contrast her view to your own? What are your problem-solving skills that work the best for you? What different skills do you need depending on whether the problem is clear-cut or messy? When you are reasoning, what deductive thinking strategies do you like to use?

There are a multitude of skills and strategies that each of us uses in different situations and in different ways. The benefit of considering these critical thinking strategies and skills in relation to collaborative partnerships is that we tend to have very individual thinking plans. Combining these plans can only work to shed more light on any project and add texture to your conversation.

And lastly, Halpern suggests that we consider *if we have reached our goal.* This is an interesting point to ponder for a collaborative experience. Success might not look like you or your partners thought it would. Unpredictable outcomes may be no less desirable than prescribed results, but it may take an attitude adjustment to consider your outcome "successful" if you are surprised by it. Perhaps a worthy question might be to ask what you learned about working collaboratively that will inform your next collaborative experience. Also, you might consider what you learned about your quest that can be used as you study this issue again.

Let Go

When teachers can "let go," they can experience both the terror or fear of lack of control as well as the exhilaration that is created in collaborating.
—Practitioner

A critical thinker will not be personally critical to collaborative partners. However, she might be an active thinker who is very directed and does not shy away from analysis and decision making. There are times when conversations can get so far off-task that collaborative partners may wonder about the time and the direction of the experience. While a certain amount of off-task conversation is needed to help the partners learn about each other, critical thinking skills come in handy to get us back on track. Collaborative partners who exercise their critical thinking skills act as "critical friends" and tend to feel that their time is well spent as they learn from each other as thoughtful professionals. As Halpern suggests, critical thinking skills are useless if they are not used. As you continue to have collaborative experiences that present you with opportunities to hone your critical thinking strategies, you will be rewarded by outcomes that demonstrate the strength of this type of thinking. For much more information about critical friends groups, search for the work of Theodore R. Sizer and the Coalition of Essential Schools. The information is easy to find, abundant, and very thought-provoking.

CREATIVE THINKING

It probably does not come as news to you that creativity is not a highly valued concept in American education. Most of us have seen the term only in a context that is designed for gifted education or as a descriptor for gifted and talented students. Creative thinking is not something, however, that is relegated to a few. All of us are capable of creative thinking. The research on creativity usually focuses on the *Big C's* (as per Howard Gardner) or the *capital C's* (as per Mihaly Csikszentmihalyi). The rest of us *little c's* have to rely mostly on current research about creating environments that enhance creativity.

An interesting juxtaposition is presented by comparing problem solving and creative thinking. Consider that creative types are those who practice their creativity regularly and that the strategies and skills that are used in problem solving are akin to thinking creatively. Now we are getting on more familiar turf. When we brainstorm and allow for all ideas, when we think in unusual ways looking at things straight on, from the sides, on top, underneath, and through, we start to open our possibilities. Divergent thinking is usually considered original or creative as opposed to convergent thinking, which leads to solutions. Why can't directed thinking include creative thinking skills? Collaborative partnerships benefit from educators who feel comfortable with both of these seemingly contradictory approaches.

Just as critical thinking implies directed, reasoned thinking, creative thinking implies not only unusual and original but also appropriate thinking. Ideas that are not appropriate for the situation are not creative. This then puts some onus on the partnership or the collaborative group

to have a consensus of what is appropriate. One hopes they will have a broad view that will encourage creative approaches.

Creative thinking enthusiasts have produced a number of thought-provoking "creative thinking checklists" to stimulate flexibility and fluidity in thinking. A famous checklist from the 1950s endures based on its general use in many situations (Whiting in Halpern, 1996, p. 384):

✓ *Put to Other Uses?* New ways to use as is? Other uses if modified?

✓ *Adapt?* What else is like this? What other idea does this suggest? Does the past offer a parallel? What could I copy? Whom could I emulate?

✓ *Modify?* New twist? Change meaning, color, motion, odor, form, shape? Other changes?

✓ *Magnify?* What to add? More time? Greater frequency? Stronger? Larger? Thicker? Extra value? Plus ingredient? Duplicate? Multiply? Exaggerate?

✓ *Minify?* What to substitute? Smaller? Condensed? Miniature? Lower? Shorter? Lighter? Omit? Streamline? Split up? Understate?

✓ *Substitute?* Who else instead? What else instead? Other ingredient? Other material? Other process? Other power? Other place? Other approach? Other tone of voice?

✓ *Rearrange?* Interchange components? Other pattern? Other layout? Other sequence? Transpose cause and effect? Change pace? Change schedule?

✓ *Reverse?* Transpose positive and negative? How about opponents? Turn it backward? Turn it upside down? Reverse roles? Change shoes? Turn tables? Turn the other cheek?

✓ *Combine?* How about a blend, an alloy, an assortment, an ensemble? Combine units? Combine purposes? Combine appeals? Combine ideas?

The value of the checklists like the one above is that they might help to spur ideas when they do not seem to be coming trippingly off the tongue. Strategies that are considered relevant to creative thinking include brainstorming, considering connections and patterns, visualizing, using metaphors and analogies, listing attributes, and using checklists like the one offered above.

The thinking skills framework that we used in our critical thinking discussion can be applied to creative thinking as well. First, the *goal* in creative thinking is to produce an original (and appropriate) approach to

a problem or situation. Second, creativity is based within a domain, and knowledge about content and background is just as important when thinking creatively; you have to *know your givens*. Third, the *skills* you use in creative thinking are where the creativity really comes alive. You will use different skills depending upon the situation. Working collaboratively can only enhance all the partners' creativity if the environment has been established that encourages and rewards mental risk taking. And lastly, the question of *reaching the goal* is addressed. Creative thinking is judged on both originality and appropriateness. The cyclical nature of the creative thinking process is akin to the collaborative process. At any point an evaluation of the outcome may send the process back to an earlier step for review and reflection.

Creative thinking is one of the fringe benefits of the collaborative process. With more than one perspective and backgrounds in bodies of knowledge, collaborative partnerships provide a rich forum for enhancing creative thought. An attitude that welcomes all ideas—including some that are riskier than others—and an environment that makes partners feel safe to share unusual ideas add texture to your partnership. And, as it does in so many other ways, your collaborative partnerships with other educators model thinking and learning behaviors that you can incorporate into the classroom. We are all much more confident transferring skills and strategies that we have actually practiced ourselves. How better to develop a learning environment that enhances creativity than to experience one yourself as an active partner?

HABITS OF MIND

In the teaching profession certain terms are batted about that help to identify how an educator might approach something new. *Attitude, orientation, professionalism, beliefs* and *perceptions* are all terms that we hear and wonder where and how we fit into these categories. There is so much room for subjectivity and personality within these types of distinctions that the entire discussion feels like we are standing on shifting sands. Attitudes and such go in and out of fashion, and then we get those recurring themes that resurface with a new moniker every twenty years.

To avoid these shifting sands and fashionable theories, we tend to stick to something that we can sink our teeth into and feel secure that we are focusing on matters of the mind and not the heart or personality of the educator. We all recognize that we have habits in our lives that subconsciously help us perform routine tasks. The same is true in our daily mental lives, both as educators and as educated adults in society. These mental habits develop over a long period of time, and they tend to ori-

ent us toward thinking in certain ways. Habits of mind are considered important in science and technology, arts and music education, and mathematics—basically, any arena where a trained mind will help the learner think through novel situations and problems as they arise. Likewise, habits of mind that orient a collaborative partner toward thinking that is productive will help the collaborative experience move forward while remaining open to challenges and opportunities along the way.

As models to our students and fellow educators, we acknowledge that we cannot teach our students everything and cannot foresee every contingency. And, of course, as educated adults we already have established mental habits that we don't tend to think about in an explicit way. As we participate in collaborative partnerships, however, we are encouraged to think about those effective habits of mind that help us to become more self-aware learners. The actual habits that we have developed may vary. There are approximately thirty to forty habits of mind that can be found by searching educational documents published online and in print in just the last few years. Art Costa, from California State University, continues to conduct extensive research in this area. Other researchers are also identifying mental habits that help learners to become more self-regulated and productive.

For our purposes, we have discussed those habits of mind that lend themselves to developing collaborative partnerships and modeling yourself as active learners:

> *Metacognition*—self-awareness of your own thinking. Planning your thinking strategies based on your knowledge and your awareness of available resources. Continually re-evaluating your position and the effectiveness of your strategy. Plan and change your plans as you consider more effective strategies. Evaluate and continue to re-evaluate your progress. Question what "progress" means within the context of each situation.

> *Mindfulness*—keeping yourself open to challenges and opportunities as they come your way. Both being in the moment and being aware of yourself as an active thinker in that moment. Think holistically, look for patterns, and break down ideas into manageable categories. Consider new information to be the beginning of new categories of thought.

> *Critical thinking*—accuracy and attention to "the text" or evidence is important. Ask yourself, "How do I know this?" and question the source and the author's motivation. Consider the scientific mind-set, where a healthy informed skepticism is necessary when learning about alternative concepts (which in science just means that the concepts have yet

to be disproved). Listening attentively to others and their perspectives helps you to understand different viewpoints. Pose new questions and ask questions about new solutions.

Creative thinking—always trying to see beyond the standard scope of an issue or a situation. Being curious and thinking flexibly. Pushing yourself to use all of your knowledge and abilities without knowing the outcome. Asking "What if?" Feeling a sense of wonder. And using humor while persevering and trusting yourself to know what your limits are. Honoring ongoing, generative modes of thought and fearlessly facing the consequences of your creative thinking.

Once you start to consider that you, too, have habits of mind and start to recognize them, you will progress in your self-awareness as a thinker. This realization will help you to form the language that you need to begin talking about yourself as a thinker. We need a language to describe our thought processes with our partners. Once we have a common language that we can share, our collaborative experiences will deepen and we will feel stronger, both as individual thinkers and as partners. Identifying our habits of mind helps us to see ourselves as lifelong learners, and we can then, in turn, model ourselves for our students and fellow educators.

SOCIAL JUSTICE

What is it about collaborative partnerships among educators that brings social justice to mind? Collaboration is a goal-oriented relationship. It is an ongoing process that progresses from discussion to action. It provides a respectful forum that welcomes the voices and perspectives of all members of the partnership. It honors the responsibilities that each member carries and the various abilities that each member brings to the partnership. The unpredictable outcomes are generative and are products of change within the group. The collaborative partnership encourages us to look within ourselves in order to be honest and forthright members of the partnership. We grow and change as learners and educators through the process of collaboration. Sounds like a healthy foundation for a socially just society, doesn't it?

Social justice has been a theme in education from John Dewey to Maxine Greene to William Ayers. As Ayers writes in the foreword to *Teaching for Social Justice* (1998), a problem for education has been its proximity to schools: "Education, of course, lives an excruciating paradox precisely because of its association with and location in schools. Education is about opening doors, opening minds, opening possibilities.

School is too often about sorting and punishing, grading and ranking and certifying. . . . Education frees the mind, while schooling bureaucratizes the brain. An educator unleashes the unpredictable, while a schoolteacher sometimes starts with an unhealthy obsession with a commitment to classroom management and linear lesson plans" (p. xxiii).

However much we agree with Ayers in sentiment, we do live in the real world, and our school learning environments are our microcosms. We cannot expect to have collaborative partnerships for every unit we teach, but it is possible for much of what we learn through these experiences to find its way into our classrooms. Of course, what you learn about content will be incorporated into your teaching. But think also about what you learn about yourself and others and the learning experience you shared. Did it help you to understand others? Did it help you to become a better listener? Did it teach you anything about working together toward a shared vision? What was it about your collaborative experience that you value the most? Perhaps it is learning about yourself so that you can understand that which you would like to change and that which you value most. Or perhaps it is learning how to be a leader and a follower and a partner with colleagues and how we are all able to learn about ourselves and each other, converse, act, and produce an outcome that simply could not have been produced alone.

There is a misconception about collaborative experiences that they are all smooth and effortless and congenial, that all the partners are friends, and that their collaboration is merely an excuse to work together. While that could be the reality and it sometimes does exist, it is certainly not always the case, and it is not necessarily desired. Consider that the basis of any collaborative experience is the relationship among professional educators who have diverse experiences and backgrounds. All relationships have ups and downs, and they are not always smooth sailing. Sometimes the experience that has had obstacles to progress feels the most rewarding in the end. Collaborative partnerships can overcome misunderstandings and can absorb multiple perspectives and variations of goals. The desire to be productive within the partnership and to generate an outcome serves to moderate the dissonance and helps partners to focus on the group goals.

Frontal Teaching

True changes come when teaching is viewed in new ways, when activities and lessons are planned to engage students, and this is not quiet or clean, nor is it only frontal teaching. This is not to say that accountability is forgotten, but figuring out ways to accomplish educational goals in pedagogically sound ways must be applauded. Similarly, in this day of standards and high-stakes testing, teachers have to see that they are valued and rewarded for trying new models of teaching and learning.–*Teacher Educator*

There is no greater teacher than action. In the collaborative partnership you are all in it together (whether you tend to agree on everything or not), and that is a very supportive way to learn. A collaborative experience that results in any one partner feeling unsatisfied is a professional life lesson for all the partners. Just as we learn from our mistakes in our personal lives, we learn from (and about) ourselves and our colleagues in this professional relationship. What we choose to do with this newly found self-knowledge is up to each of us. Most often there are some rewards from the collaborative experience, and the generative nature of the process pushes (pulls?) us into another experience with a better understanding of collaboration and all of its variables.

The social justice implications of educator collaboration are simple. Educators are, on the whole, a hopeful lot. We believe in a brighter future, and moreover, we believe that we have a role in that future. Our students are our future. Anything we can do to influence that future generation to work and live together in harmony, in a more socially just and democratic society, is within our purview as educators. Clearly, the world our children will inherit is one in which social justice is no longer an abstract notion touted by the liberal-minded, but it is now an essential principle for the global society to co-exist. What better way for us to learn firsthand how to work together than to have our own collaborative partnerships to guide us so that we can become models for our students and other members of our learning community. What more "real world" impact can our practice have than to help us teach that change is possible when we listen to and learn about ourselves and others and act together toward a mutually agreed upon goal?

CHAPTER 7

Educator Collaboration: A Framework and Reflections

A framework is just that. It is a skeleton-like structure of ideas and actions that are designed to be implemented by practitioners who will fill out the design. The framework that is presented here is a sketch. Some parts of it will be more applicable than others in different school learning environments. It is not a linear pathway like a flowchart. It is a cyclical process that generates additional collaborative relationships and projects. Following each section are questions and comments posed by the experts who were instrumental in revising the framework from a research project to a useful tool for understanding educator collaboration. Use them as discussion prompts or as reflective prompts for writing.

This framework has a variety of purposes:

- It presents a common language that we may share when discussing collaboration.

- It provides a blueprint for developing a collaborative relationship.

- It prompts discussion by those who find themselves in a mandated collaborative group but do not know where to start.

- It suggests to administrators that supporting collaborative relationships is not as simple as providing common prep time.

- It is a dynamic tool designed to get you talking and sharing and thinking about how each of the conditions relates to you.

- It is a malleable construct. The framework itself is not etched in stone. *Use what fits and throw out the rest; better yet, re-write it to suit your situation.*

You might want to photocopy the framework with one section per page to leave room for reflective notes or to discuss one section at each initial meeting of a new collaborative group. You might want to lift the framework out so that everyone in the group reads it all before you meet for the first time so that you start off with a common language.

Approach the framework with the idea that it is a tool for you to use in the most suitable way for your purposes. Abraham Maslow commented that if every tool is a hammer, then every problem is a nail. If every educator's toolkit includes a framework of collaboration, then some problems will benefit from the efforts of a goal-oriented collaborative relationship. Experience teaches us which tools to use; all we need to do is have them available to us so that we are well prepared for whatever might come along.

WHY ARE WE DISCUSSING COLLABORATION IN THE SCHOOLS?

There is no doubt that collaboration is in the spotlight in education. The term is showing up everywhere, including standards for general education teachers (INTASC, 1992), reading specialists (IRA, 1998), school librarians (AASL & AECT, 1998a), and special education teachers (CEC, 1998). There is a growing body of literature, including books and articles written for both academic and practitioner audiences. In all of the above cases, an assumption is made that we are all poised and ready to dive into collaboration. It appears that there is very little energy going into instruction to prepare educators for collaborative experiences.

A Healthy School

The task of improving schools today may be integral to the task of developing collaboration. A healthy school is one characterized by relatedness between people and professionals seeking intellectual gratification from others and from the work itself.

—Administrator

Like everything else in life, some of us may feel that we come by this stance more naturally than others do. Regardless, we need a common language so that all educators in the school will be able to share experiences and grow together as a learning community. And every educator needs the same chance at success in every aspect of teaching, just like we all agree that we need to give every student an equal chance to learn. We can all use a relevant and practical tool that will further the dialogue about working together as partners in the schools.

So, this framework starts out one giant step before the stance. The goal is to build a common ground for collaboration that can be used by every specialized area within education. It provides a place to begin the conversation and, we hope, establish a level playing field for collaboration for all of us in the schools. We find that by collaborating with our colleagues, we focus on our strengths and better serve all of our students.

The theory that supports this framework was based on approximately 600 collaborative experiences in a high school over a five-year period.

Practitioners (classroom teachers and reading, special education, bilingual, and school library media specialists), administrators, teacher educators, national organization executives, and policymakers then reviewed a draft of this framework and made both specific recommendations and general comments about educator collaboration. These participants represent a range of specialties from early childhood to post-secondary practitioners; teacher education programs; administration at all levels, including principals and superintendents; city, regional, and state education programs; school reformers and educational research consultants; and national teacher education and staff development professional organizations. This revised framework reflects the suggestions of this wide array of education practitioners and scholars. It is hoped that this framework will encourage teachers to have new insights into themselves and their colleagues as active, reflective learners and will encourage us all to partner together to improve both student and teacher learning. Use this framework as a place to begin the conversation.

FRAMEWORK OF EDUCATOR COLLABORATION

What Is Basic to All Aspects of Collaboration?

TRUST AND RESPECT permeate all professional interactions of value in the schools. Without mutual trust and respect, classroom teachers and resource educators have no basis for goal-oriented collaboration. We can be both independent and trusting professionals. Educators who collaborate have trust and respect for ourselves, our students, our colleagues, and our entire school community.

Defining the Phenomenon

Working together draws on teachers' areas of strength; it provides for new levels of reflective discussion about what makes for effective teaching and authentic learning.

–Teacher Educator

What Needs to Be in Place for Collaboration to Occur?

INDIVIDUALITY or a sense of oneself as an independent thinker with an intact professional identity is a key ingredient. Educators who have deep content knowledge, who value preparedness and respect for students, enjoy an independent sense of confidence. Trust and respect are not only for others but for ourselves as worthy of empowerment, with ownership over one's body of work; then it moves to our students and our colleagues as we find collaborative partners who share these professional values. **LEADERSHIP** is a key element, but it is the **BALANCE** of being able to follow as your collaborative partner leads that is equally important. A shared vision and shared goals ensure that collaborative partners balance their leadership, their individuality or independence, and their interdependence. What needs to be in place for collaboration to occur resides within each of us. Then trust and respect pave the way.

Significant Leader

It really does take a significant leader to change school culture–someone who can give space when it is needed and pressure as well, someone who is good at clarifying the purpose of a collaborative culture, someone who is trying to focus on a few well-chosen goals.–*Policymaker*

How Do We Define "Educator Collaboration"?

First, let's distinguish **COLLABORATION** from compromise, cooperation, and coordination. What sets collaboration apart from these other forms of interaction is that the outcome is greater than the sum of the parts. In compromise, cooperation, and coordination, the sum of the parts is either less (compromise) or the same as it would be without the interaction. Teachers who share lesson plans, "I'll show you mine if you show me yours," call cooperation collaboration. Many of us cooperate with each other, but moving beyond cooperation is more challenging. Collaborative experiences lead to outcomes that are greater than the partners could have achieved as independents. The outcomes are also often unpredictable and sometimes unintended. The end result is one that is somehow surprisingly larger than life. Even the process of collaboration is one that affords results that enlighten and touch the partners in unexpected ways. The partners learn that their strengths as individuals and leaders serve them well when dealing with the unexpected. As we observe and share with others, we find ourselves reflecting on our own practice. The collaborative experience then serves to further strengthen those aspects of our professional identities that we value, and we find ourselves seeking future partnerships and collaborative efforts that reflect those strengths.

From Cooperation to Collaboration

It is extremely difficult to move beyond cooperation to collaboration. It can take years, and even committed and well-meaning individuals can rarely accomplish and/or maintain true collaboration. True collaborative behavior requires time for individual work, time for interaction, time for reflection, and time for redirection. It also requires a significant amount of energy.—*Policymaker*

What Type of School Environment Fosters Collaboration?

Collaboration thrives in an environment of **COMMUNITY.** In a way, this is a cyclical argument because collaborative experiences also help to build a supportive, caring community spirit. So, prior experiences and support for collaboration from colleagues and administrators nurture partnerships. A caring community that embraces shared visions and goals, respect for students, sensitivity, evaluation, spirit, time, pleasure, and celebration provides a **HOLISTIC ENVIRONMENT** for the whole student *and* the whole educator. Can collaborative experiences occur in non-supportive environments? Yes. Can community sometimes become exclusive and non-nurturing? Yes. Challenges in the school environment determine the amount of time and energy and inventiveness necessary to have effective collaborative experiences. Goals must be firmly intact to overcome environmental obstacles.

Equity

Think about equity with regard to involvement . . . People have different expectations and often don't talk about the issues. So what are the issues of equity in collaboration when power differentials are there? Gender, status, race, ethnicity, etc.—*Teacher Educator*

What Other Factors in the School May Impact Collaboration?

There are other factors in the environment of a school that are broader and relate to all of our experiences in education. **STRUCTURE, TIME,** and **CLASSROOM MANAGEMENT** are a few universal school factors that we all share. We may feel pressure from some or all of these factors, or we may actually find opportunities hiding in unexpected places. Collaboration does take time, especially at the beginning stages. As the collaborative process evolves, a new sense of time emerges. Suddenly, time for collaborative work, interactions, reflection, and redirection is carved out of the school day. Classroom dynamics change when another educator enters the picture. Collaborative experiences have the power to hold some of these factors aloft so that we perceive them in different ways than we did when we faced them alone. Standards actually have a way of bringing educators together to share perspectives and insights. You might find that conversations with colleagues take on a new tone that bends time. When educators experience the results of shared responsibilities and time saved because of a true partnership, these factors can shift in importance. This element requires an open mind and a fresh approach to preconceived notions of barriers and boundaries.

Flow

The sense of flow that comes from good collaboration happens because the participants have a common clearly structured goal and clear feedback as to whether they are achieving that goal or not.–*Practitioner*

What Strategies Go into the Collaborative Process?

Educator collaboration is not another "package" that requires strategies and procedures that operate in isolation of the school day. Do you think **CREATIVELY** and **CRITICALLY,** and are you an **ACTIVE, REFLECTIVE LEARNER?** You will find that collaboration generates even more creativity because another perspective will enrich your learning. As you begin to dialogue with colleagues, share critiques of your work, observe each other in action, and share a willingness to change and grow, you will find communication strategies that work for you in your particular situation. Generosity, preparedness, trust, and respect combine with creativity to produce a **SYNERGY** that true collaborative partners enjoy. Authentic learning, modeling, engaged learning, and community of learners probably cause you to think about teaching strategies. Take a moment to consider yourself as the learner. Participate in these strategies, and you will then create deeper, richer learning experiences for your students based on your own experiences as learners. You will explore messy, ill-defined problems and will need to engage in problem resolution that will intrigue you as you learn more about yourself as a thinker and a learner. This is a fine way to find a partner and start your collaborative process as active learners. You will learn to appreciate our different perspectives and honor our varied strengths.

Holistic Endeavors

Some good collaborators come out of nonsupportive environments. People can collaborate in environments that are pretty repellant to holistic endeavors—because they have a mutual goal.
—*Teacher Educator*

What Outcomes Are Expected with Educator Collaboration?

Since this is a creative process and you will be redirecting your path along the way, the results are by definition **UNPREDICTABLE** and often **UNINTENDED.** Your shared vision and goals will direct your activities, but you cannot anticipate a predictable outcome.

You CAN expect

> **We, Not Me**
>
> When the educators/collaborators can really believe in *we*, not *me*, the power is extraordinary . . . It is through understanding the process of collaboration that this faith is further developed and trusted, and institutional change becomes reality.
> —*Practitioner*

☆ to be surprised and feel celebratory when you experience creative consequences that are fresh, real, and transformative;

☆ new memories in your life as a learner that will have deep roots and will reach great heights;

☆ deeply experienced, textured, generative outcomes that will most certainly give you incentive to reflect on your practice;

☆ your students to have unique learning experiences that develop from your collaborative efforts with colleagues; and

☆ the most powerful result of all, *the impetus to initiate another experience in the ongoing process of collaboration and self-discovery.*

FRAMEWORK REFLECTIONS

Throughout this book, you have been reading comments made by the educators who participated in revising the framework. The following reflections are organized along the framework elements and further illuminate their points of consensus and disagreement.

Do not use these reflections to override your own perspectives or that of your collaborative partner(s). Just add them to the mix.

Of all the elements discussed in the framework, the causal condition of *individuality* stands out as the most intriguing. Research found that the importance of a sense of individuality and/or professional identity is a key ingredient for collaboration to occur. Some experts in the education field contend that this concept is "counterintuitive," and others claim that it is an "aha" experience for them to contemplate. Others state that they felt that individuality was understood as critically important for any collegial relationship. The greatest perceived hindrance to collaboration within the schools is the isolationistic culture of teaching. So, it appears that both isolation and collaboration are dependent on like elements for effective teaching! It is also interesting to note that standards and the emphasis on test scores while seemingly stripping teachers of their autonomy actually may encourage teachers to collaborate for shared insights and to develop new behaviors that accommodate these changes. According to some administrator contributors, the accountability that teachers now face is more confidently and comfortably faced when they work together as partners.

Deeply Felt . . . Richly Textured

How does the description of collaborative outcomes as deeply felt and richly textured help people to plan and encourage collaboration? The impact of collaboration is long term and often not immediately tangible. Districts should value collaboration for the way it enriches individual teaching and teaching communities. Collaborating teachers are better teachers than they would otherwise have been.
—*Practitioner*

The emphasis on *balance* in the discussion of leadership is also of particular interest. Anyone who has worked professionally with others knows that in a group of two or more, not everyone can lead at all times. It takes a true leader to know when not to lead. The business field has leadership motivational books galore extolling the virtues of leaders who have this skill.

Collaboration, as it was *defined* in this framework, leads to the context and vice versa. This is an example of the recursive nature of this phenomenon. The concept of *context* as one of a caring community emerged as a strong element in the paradigm. Those educators who

collaborate seem to consider the entire school to be their responsibility and not just what occurs in their classrooms. This perception of school as community lends itself to a collaborative environment, and conversely, a collaborative environment helps to establish a perception of a school learning community where all students "belong to" all the adults in the school.

Broad conditions that impact all schools, such as *time, structure,* and *classroom management,* need to be addressed in any discussion of educator collaboration. The viewpoint that these intervening conditions are insurmountable obstacles is a personal perception held by some (most?) educators. Some contributors remarked about the relative nature of *time.* Of course, there is agreement that the most important commodity to teachers is time and that collaboration takes time. There are those who question the effectiveness of their time management and priorities. The negative impact of administrative duties on teachers' time is a strongly held perception. One wonders at the lack of teacher support in this area. Many other professionals have clerical assistance with paperwork. It could be argued that teachers should have teacher assistants who would be responsible for much of the administrative work in the same way that paralegals function in a law firm. Traditionally, paraprofessionals in schools are assigned to monitor and supervise students. Perhaps their responsibilities could be broadened to absorb those duties that keep teachers from more professional responsibilities. The gift of time is not always a guarantee of collaboration. Sometimes stolen moments heighten the value of a shared goal and could cause teachers to feel more intrinsically rewarded for their collaborative efforts.

> ### Strategies
>
> Besides generosity and preparedness: dialogue, critique, willingness to change–TRUST.
> *–Teacher Educator*

Many teachers are creative, and their students benefit from their teachers' innovative teaching styles. Still, we each have only one person's perspective, talents, and ingenuity to depend upon. The *synergism* that takes over a well-oiled collaborative effort takes on a life of its own. Projects have a way of seeming like they are organic when they are the kind that ignite the imagination and force us to think in new and different ways. Teachers who share this feeling with a collaborative partner develop a sense of camaraderie and enriched professional satisfaction. Some of that exuberance comes from the feeling of learning something so new and relating it to prior knowledge, fitting it into new situations, and taking joint ownership of the learning process. It seems to follow that teachers will then want their students to experience the same elation in collaborative projects in the curriculum.

The *outcomes* of educator collaboration, then, are often unpredictable. Whereas we have control over our own knowledge base and willingness to delve into it, we do not have that control over others'. As we co-mingle our efforts, each of us controls only ourselves. Therefore,

we are unable to predict what an outcome of mixed efforts might look like. Granted, it might not be what we had intended, but it might far surpass our expectations. Once again, a creative mind is believed to be a plus when managing and handling unexpected consequences. As we effectively manage the formerly unmanageable ill-defined problems, and we enjoy the sensation of accomplishment, we want to raise the challenge to a new level. In that way, the consequences of a collaborative effort feed into the next occurrence. It is teacher "flow." One can imagine a spiral comprised of ever-rising collaborative learning processes.

Time

Time in our culture has its own particular meaning and importance.
—Teacher Educator

The following are highlights of the framework according to the practitioners who contributed their input:

- Shared goals so that the collaboration is clearly goal-oriented.
- Choosing to collaborate as opposed to being assigned.
- Structures can create opportunity with the right frame of mind.
- Ability and challenge to reflect on one's own practices.
- Time bends.
- The accountability born of standards is not considered to be an obstacle but rather a boon to collaboration.

All things considered, it is fair to say that there was overwhelming support for this framework by the contributors and concurrence that collaboration is not addressed explicitly in either teacher education or most professional development programs and needs to be. The framework was viewed as a comprehensive tool designed to enhance our understanding of the phenomenon of the collaboration process in the schools. As one contributing practitioner wrote, "In your model I tried to find one thought, one point, one theory that was not there based on *my* experience. I could find none!" It seems that the theory written in the form of a framework could meet the needs of diverse practitioners.

Framework of Educator Collaboration contributors saw different sides of this phenomenon depending on their various vantage points:

> **Practitioners** saw the framework and related to their unique situations.

> **Administrators** saw burnt-out veteran teachers and their concept of time as a formidable challenge.

> **Teacher educators** saw the advantage of teachers understanding differences among themselves and appreciating those differences.

Policymakers reported their approval of the definition of collaboration offered and commented on the interesting paradox of the importance of "individuality" in collaboration; they emphasized the concept of teachers as leaders and warned against a self-defeating "too-deep foundation" that might stifle creativity.

We have a structure in place, we have considered various perspectives, and now we are ready to dive into educator collaboration in the next chapter. The framework that has been presented is just an outline for you to fill in. The experts' viewpoints are there for your perusal but are not edicts from on high. Integrate what you have read and considered into your own unique situation. Take what works for you and leave the rest behind for someone else. It is time to begin your own beginnings and prepare to reflect upon your own collaborative experiences.

CHAPTER **8**

The School Buddy System

By heaven, methinks it were an easy leap
To pluck bright honour from the pale-faced moon,
Or dive into the bottom of the deep,
Where fathom line could never touch the ground,
And pluck up drowned honour by the locks,
So he that doth redeem her thence might wear
Without corrival all her dignities...

—Shakespeare, *1 Henry IV*, Act I, Scene III

So muses Hotspur in *The First Part of the History of King Henry IV* (Shakespeare, 1597/1980, p. 19): "Methinks it were an easy leap." If it were an easy leap to dive into the bottom of the deep, we would not be taking that giant step back from the edge of the water. All that would be necessary would be willing, knowledgeable parties; a suitable context; and favorable intervening conditions. New standards are calling for collaboration among teachers, and there are schools where time is designated in the school day for that purpose. The National Board for Professional Teaching Standards (NBPTS) includes collaboration in each type of certificate. For example, according to the *2000–2001 Guide to National Board Certification* (2000a), one of the eleven standards for the "Early Adolescence/Generalist" certificate is entitled, "Collaboration with Colleagues." The description of this standard reads, "Accomplished generalists work with colleagues to improve schools and to advance knowledge and practice in their field" (p. 37). One of the five core propositions that are the basis for National Board certification is that "teachers are members of learning communities" (2000b, p. 3). It appears that positive steps are being taken to facilitate educator collaboration.

WHAT, THEN, IS AT ISSUE?

In truth, even with considerable effort from supportive administrators, many educators still do not find this to be an easy leap. In their book, *The Teaching Gap: Best Ideas from the World's Teachers for Improving Education in the Classroom,* Stigler and Hiebert (1999) ask, "Once a district has laid out an organizational structure for school improvement, with time for teachers to work in collaborative groups, what should teachers do with their newfound time? Many reformers who thought increased planning time, by itself, would lead to improvements in teaching have found that it does not. Indeed, teachers who are told simply to collaborate often find that they are not sure what they are supposed to do, or how such collaborations can help them to improve their teaching" (p. 149). The authors do not offer any guidance beyond making this claim. Elmore, Peterson, and McCarthey (1996) also found that even schools that attempt reforms use teachers' (discretionary) time in ways that do not improve classroom practices.

> **AMAZINGLY INDEPENDENT**
>
> Teachers are amazingly independent or individual. Usually it is when they are alone or perhaps because they are alone. When a teacher first starts teaching, one of the reasons to collaborate is to share lessons or preparation. The collaboration in shared preparation feels somewhat akin to competition. So can collaboration exist without competition? –Practitioner

The argument for instructing teachers for collaboration (as it is presented in this book) assumes that the education community agrees that collaboration improves student learning. Not only is this not the case but policymakers by their nature are reluctant to entertain collaboration seriously because of the complicated nature of the process itself. One policymaker who contributed his comments to this book is the former commissioner of the National Center for Educational Statistics (NCES); he agrees that collaboration is timely—in some education circles. But he laments, "Unfortunately, it is often not among the primary interests of policymakers or in conversations between educators and policymakers. Collaboration takes time and effort, and its results . . . are unpredictable; the strong predilection of policymakers is toward simple and popular ideas, many of which make no lasting change or simply do not create the promised change." Another skeptical viewpoint comes from a contributor who is an educational anthropologist who has worked closely on Chicago school reforms. He argues, "The fundamental culture of schooling mitigates against such an approach."

It would be possible to just sweep these contrary views under the rug since national standards for content area classroom teachers, special

**The
End in Mind**

It is my experience in special education that standards can actually provide an
impetus for collaboration. I have seen this to
be true in states where standards are used for
planning and preparation. Grant Wiggins eludes to
this with his backward design, or planning with the
end in mind. The standards can bring teachers
together to plan joint units about how to best
meet the standards or to create an evaluation from which the instructional design
can be created and implemented.
–Practitioner

education teachers, reading specialists, and school library media specialists have current standards that all include collaboration as a guiding principle (INTASC, 1992; AASL & AECT, 1998a; CEC, 1998; IRA, 1998; NBPTS, 2000a). Moot point notwithstanding, these are issues that must be faced if we are to explore collaboration in the schools in a meaningful way.

A few proponents of educator collaboration have been busy improving schools through their own research efforts. Deborah Meier's work at Central Park East, Theodore R. Sizer's Coalition of Essential Schools movement, and Linda Darling-Hammond's work with the National Center for Restructuring Education, Schools, and Teaching (NCREST) all speak to issues of school culture, change, and collaboration in education. In *The Power of Their Ideas: Lessons for America from a Small School in Harlem,* Meier (1995) describes qualities that she looks for in prospective teachers, including "(1) a self-conscious reflectiveness about how they themselves learn and (maybe even more) about how and when they *don't* learn; (2) a sympathy toward others, an appreciation of differences, an ability to imagine one's own 'otherness'; (3) a willingness, better yet *a taste,* for working collaboratively; (4) a passion for having others share some of one's own interests; and then (5) a lot of perseverance, energy, and devotion to getting things right!" (p. 142). Meier reflects that finding all five of these qualities is unlikely, so administrators need to create the schools that will draw them out.

Horace's Hope: What Works for the American High School is the second in Sizer's (1996) Horace Smith trilogy. Reflecting on "What Matters," Sizer writes, *"Human-scale places are critical.* . . . Sharing knowledge about kids requires trusting colleagueship among teachers. When we are chosen to work in a school on the basis of a commitment to the philosophy of that school and because our arrival will strengthen the corps of staff members already there, the relationship of each of us to the others is always crucial, particularly so if the school is taking on tough reforms" (pp. 91-92). In Coalition of Essential Schools, culture of the school is as critical as human scale. Sizer suggests that in Essential Schools "teachers are expected to consult with one another, and easy relationships among colleagues—formal or informal, as the individuals like—are the norm. . . . Where teachers are full of questions about ideas, where they talk about them—heatedly argue about them—among themselves . . . the effect is real" (p. 93).

Darling-Hammond (1997) suggests what teachers need to know and be able to do in *The Right to Learn: A Blueprint for Creating Schools That Work.* She enumerates those factors as subject content knowledge, pedagogical content knowledge, child development, culture differences, motivation, learning, and the ability to assess students' knowledge and approaches to learning. Additionally, Darling-Hammond reports "teachers need to know about *collaboration.* They need to understand how to collaborate with other teachers to plan, assess, and improve learning within the school and also how to work with parents to learn more about individual children and to shape supportive experiences at school and home" (p. 297).

Darling-Hammond suggests that the goal of education policymaking should be to "develop the capacity of schools and teachers to create practices that reflect what is now known about effective ways to teach and learn" (p. 332). Stating this goal belies the controversy of the reputation of educational research and its impact, or lack thereof, on policymaking (Kaestle, 1993; Sroufe, 1997). Darling-Hammond contends that initiatives are needed to help develop policies that support constructivistic school cultures, where practice is learner-centered. One of those initiatives recommends that policies must address changes in teacher education. Teachers must be helped to "acquire the knowledge they need to teach powerfully . . . this includes the capacity to work collectively and reflect on practice with other teachers. The policy goals should be to ensure that all children have access to skillful teachers, to make the teaching profession more attractive to talented young adults, and to produce humane and intellectually lively learning communities for both students and teachers" (p. 334).

> **Demonstrations of Achievement**
>
> In terms of student learning, we want to see demonstrations of achievement. In terms of teacher learning, we want to observe changes in behavior that mirror thoughtful and purposeful reflection on practice. In terms of collaborative communities, we need new ways to measure how this synergy generates creative solutions.—*Teacher Educator*

LESSON STUDY *(Jugyou Kenkyuu)*

The leading educational reformers included above are all focusing on American school cultures and teachers. In *The Teaching Gap,* Stigler and Hiebert (1999) reflect on research from the Third International Mathematics and Science Study (TIMSS). After studying videos of mathematics teachers in Germany, Japan, and the United States, the authors recommend that practices followed in Japan might stop the seemingly endless cycle of American educational reforming (Cuban, 1990). Stigler and Hiebert report that although there are individual differences among teachers, each country in the study took on general characteristics. They suggest that it is not American teachers

themselves who need revamping but American teaching methods.

In Japan, there is a culture of continuous school-based improvement that is centered in teacher inquiry groups that focus on lesson study. *Kounaikenshuu* translates into the "continuous process of school-based professional development that Japanese teachers engage in once they begin their teaching careers" (p. 110). The national curriculum in Japan mandates more standardization of practices at each grade level. Participation in professional development groups is considered to be a part of the teacher's job. The teacher's professional training is viewed as continuous throughout his or her career, unlike the four-year undergraduate teaching education requirement in the United States. These professional development groups are more commonly found in elementary and middle schools than high schools because of the emphasis on national exam matriculation in the higher grades. A common component of these groups is lesson study *(jugyou kenkyuu)*. Lesson study presents the teacher group with a manageable unit of analysis. The philosophy suggests that if the teachers want to improve learning, the most effective starting point is within the context of a classroom lesson.

> ## "I" to "We"
> The national agenda of school improvement and continuous staff development should be how we change things from "I" to "we." Unless adults talk to one another, observe one another, and help one another, very little will change. Relationships among the adults in the schools are the basis and the preconditions that allow, energize, and sustain all other attempts at school improvement.—*Administrator*

Reflecting on lesson study, Stigler and Hiebert claim that the U.S. perspective would find this approach to be too narrowly focused to be a driving force in long-term educational improvements. To refute this claim, they identify key aspects of lesson study that help to explain its impact on Japan's educational success. One of their key aspects is that "lesson study is collaborative. By working in groups to improve instruction, teachers are able to develop a shared language for describing and analyzing classroom teaching, and to teach each other about teaching" (p. 123). Stigler and Hiebert compare this perspective to the isolation of the U.S. school culture. They contend that "collaboration includes continuing interactions about effective teaching methods plus observations of one another's classrooms. These activities help teachers reflect on their own practice and identify things that can be improved . . . teacher collaboration can create a profound motivation to improve" (p. 124). Additionally, "the collaborative nature of lesson study balances the self-critiquing of individual teachers with the idea that improved teaching is a joint process, not the province or the responsibility of any individual.

This idea is embodied in the fact that when Japanese teachers plan a lesson collaboratively, they treat the result as a joint product whose ownership is shared by all in the group" (pp. 124–125). Schools, districts, and education conferences provide avenues for communicating this research throughout the Japanese educational community. The authors quote a Japanese teacher who, when asked why she invests so much effort in trying to improve lessons, replied, "If we didn't do research lessons, we wouldn't be teachers" (p. 127).

Center stage in any discussion about school reforms is student learning. Why has the discussion of improving student achievement not been the motivating force behind any alternative to traditional teaching methods? Stigler and Hiebert (1999) propose six principles used to improve teaching that, in turn, improve student achievement. Principle 5 is "Make Improvement the Work of Teachers." They claim that "one way to ensure that improvements can be developed in context is to entrust change to those engaged in the activity—classroom teachers." They go on to state emphatically that "in fact, almost all successful attempts to improve teaching have involved teachers working together to improve students' learning" (p. 135). They cite educational researchers Little and Darling-Hammond, among others, with respect to providing evidence to support this claim. Common sense tells us that group reflections on practice will offer more perspectives than self-reflections. Current educational research backs up this contention.

Common sense might also suggest that teachers who participate as learners in goal-directed learning activities with their colleagues would be in a better position to teach cooperative learning strategies in their classrooms. This is not to suggest that these strategies overwhelm all other methods, but even E. D. Hirsch, who is considered to be a staunch supporter of teacher-centered, traditional teaching methods, supports the inclusion of guided small-group work. In *The Schools We Need and Why We Don't Have Them,* Hirsch (1996) agrees that there are many roads leading to Rome. He supports "the ancient wisdom of integrating both direct and indirect methods, including inquiry learning, which encourages students to think for themselves, and direct informing, which is sometimes the most effective and efficient mode of securing knowledge and skill" (p. 174).

Mush

It is very difficult for individuals to truly collaborate or to effectively engage in developing integrated learning experiences if they do not have a deep understanding of their respective content areas. Too often, collaboration is attempted without a fundamental understanding of the subject area(s), and the result is a "mushy" project or one that simply skims the surface of a number of subject areas.—*Policymaker*

Although Hirsch argues that "the only truly general principle that seems to emerge from process-outcome research on pedagogy is that focused and guided instruction is far more effective than naturalistic, discovery, learn-at-your-own-pace instruction," he adds that "within the context of focused and guided instruction, almost anything goes, and what works best with one group of students may not work best with another group with similar backgrounds in the very same building" (p. 174). Following Hirsch's contention, the Japanese program of lesson study would serve as a natural step related to the inquiry into the best practices taking place within American classrooms. Teacher education and professional development programs could go a long way toward supporting effective teaching methods if teachers are exposed to these methods as learners themselves within the supportive professional environment of *kounaikenshuu*.

JUST ONE PIECE OF THE PUZZLE

The contents and structures of the *Framework of Educator Collaboration* can be shared with others when we are asked to collaborate with educators from various areas of specialization. It is poised to become both integrated into the larger body of work relating to collaboration in teacher education and professional development programs and generative in that those associated with specialized areas within education use it to build their own models as needed.

Those educators who are interested in studying collaboration further will find other studies that have been designed to focus on collaboration as it exists in various educational settings. This book is designed to focus on providing a foundation and a common language for veterans (experts), novices, and preservice educators to understand the elements of collaboration. I hope it will provide both a springboard and a soft landing, whatever is needed in your situation.

THE COLLABORATION CONVERSATION CONTINUES

The discussion about the process of collaboration is another tool that aids educators in understanding themselves as active learners. This view of teacher as learner is gaining ground. The Association for Supervision and Curriculum Development (ASCD) published *Educators as Learners: Creating a Professional Learning Community in Your School* (Wald & Castleberry, 2000) as a "'lesson plan' for members of a school or school system to transform their institution or organization into a learning community" (p. vi). The collaborative learning process figures prominently

 **91**

in this publication. ASCD also sends a newsletter to members. The March 2000 issue of *Education Update* features a cover story entitled "Finding Time to Collaborate" (Mann, 2000). The May 2000 issue focuses on new skills for contemporary principals. The cover story includes advice from nationally recognized principals who understand that they need to build within their teachers a desire to be empowered (Checkley, 2000). They encourage teachers to work together and to build trust. They recommend establishing a culture that supports teacher leadership and shared decision making.

Topic of Conversation

Collaboration is often not among the primary interests of policymakers or in conversations between educators and policymakers. Collaboration takes time and effort, and its results are unpredictable; the strong predilection of policymakers is toward simple and popular ideas, many of which make no lasting change or simply do not create the promised change.
—*Policymaker*

Perhaps it sounds simplistic, but collaboration in the schools generally starts with a conversation between two professionals. It is this dialogue that grows into a set of social interactions that has the potential to reward the educators with the greatest gift in their profession, a feeling of serving their students to the best of their abilities. Additional rewards may be an enriched sense of community in the school; a deeper commitment to the teaching profession; a greater sense of oneself as a learner and a teacher; a sense of oneself as a role model to the school learning community; a more textured understanding of one's own discipline and the expertise of collaborative partners; and a greater capacity to handle unintentional, unpredictable, but delightful results as a part of the collaborative learning process.

As we search for wisdom in education we understand that the dialogue is ongoing. The knowledge base for collaboration in the schools is growing. The educational research community is beginning to recognize the void of *the teacher's voice* and simultaneously beginning to value teachers' scholarship. As an example of action research, the research that led to this book could be followed by similar studies where the collaborative experiences are based in other hubs within the school. Additional studies following this research could replicate the study from the perspective of particular educators: the reading specialist, bilingual resource teacher, special education teacher, and instructional technology specialist. Our understanding of the collaborative process would be that much deeper. Other members of the school community, such as guidance counselors, school psychologists, and school social workers, and administrators could replicate similar research. An interesting study would entail interviewing administrators and practitioners at schools that are considered to be exemplars in their collaborative professional learning environment.

The bottom line for our work as educators is improving education or, more specifically, improving student achievement. Research tells us that students who are taught by teachers who have collaborated do have higher achievement rates than students taught by teachers who work alone. Any additional research in this area will encourage administrators to view collaboration as an integral part of their school learning environment, and they will restructure their schools to adjust to the requisite needs of collaborating teachers. Of course, research alone will not transform the thinking of most administrators. The research must be based in the school context and must be presented to administrators in a manner that indicates to them that their own students will benefit from any adjustment toward applying the research in their school in a measurable way.

The Power

Do not underestimate the power of attitudes, values, norms, and roles in facilitating or impeding the act of working together.—*Teacher Educator*

Just as teachers are now being encouraged to explore themselves as learners, administrators should also be encouraged to release themselves from the "we've always done it this way" manacles of education and seek understanding of recommended methods of teaching and learning to meet the needs of their school learning community. Rick DuFour, superintendent of the Stevenson High School in Lincolnshire, Illinois, claims that "it can be difficult to find time for collaboration, yet all schools can find time once they develop a shared vision of what's important" (Mann, 2000, p. 3). He reports that "we don't want people working by themselves. What's driving our time commitment is a commitment to continuous improvement. This faculty takes the notion of success for every student very seriously. That's why we value collaboration" (p. 3). Astute administrators face the formidable challenge of providing a supportive learning environment without mandating collegiality.

THE SCHOOL BUDDY SYSTEM

Collaboration buddies come in all different forms; some are classroom teachers, library media specialists, reading specialists, special education specialists, bilingual resource teachers, administrators, board members, support staff, community members, business leaders, university professors; they may reside in your building, district, community, region, across the country, around the world. Think broadly and be open; barriers and boundaries are not applicable in the quest for goal-oriented, purposeful educator collaboration.

It is my belief that collaboration between and among educators

ensures that they are continuing to reconstruct their experiences and are working together as professionals toward an education where the process and the goal are the same. Furthermore, *The School Buddy System* is not the product of a single author but a collaborative effort. I am joined by the many cited scholars, including John Dewey, Lev Vygotsky, Jerome Bruner, Vera John-Steiner, Maxine Greene, Ann L. Brown, Gary L. Anderson, and Howard Gardner; my collaborative partners at Maine West High School; and the practitioners, administrators, teacher educators, and policymakers who contributed their comments to the draft framework. It is my hope that this addition to the body of knowledge will make the conversation about collaboration in the schools a little deeper, a little more commonplace, and a little more inclusive.

The fundamental issue of collaboration in education is the same as it is in all of life. It is a part of the human condition to accept that we are all in this together. It follows, then, that we naturally achieve more together than any one of us could attain individually. And it also seems natural that sometimes, in the dark moments, life seems to be too much for any one of us to bear. The Beatles suggest that we get a little help from our friends. I suggest that when we are nearing the water's edge, we remember not to swim alone. I conclude that it is best to follow the buddy system in education, as in life.

CHAPTER **9**

Conversation Prompts

Sometimes it is hard to just get started, to stick that toe into the water; sometimes it feels a tad chilly to try to enter into a potential collaborative relationship with people that you hardly know. Familiarity is comforting, and without that, we are asking a lot of each other regardless of the profession or purpose of the collaboration.

The conversation prompts that follow are personal reflections on educator collaborative experiences over a five-year period in a public high school. Each prompt reflects on a few experiences and highlights those elements that stand out and/or those that are common.

Use these prompts however you can to enable your beginning conversations. Disagree with them, defend them against attack, compare them to your partnerships' experiences, write self-reflective journal entries, use them as prompts for discussion or brainstorming sessions.

There are forty prompts included here, one for each week of the school year. If that works for you, great. If not, figure out your own pattern. They are not sequential, so be as random as you choose. Perhaps each member of your partnership wants to report on a different reflection. Fine. These belong to you now. They are fodder for *your* thoughts.

1 ᏋᏋ Imagination Times Two

A. A PINWHEEL: TRUST AND RESPECT

Take a spin. Imagine a pinwheel with "trust" and "respect" in the middle serving as the cog pin. Without these two factors, teachers would not take the steps, would not turn in my direction, to suggest a collaborative experience. Imagine the elements needed for collaboration on each of the parts of the pinwheel. As it spins, you cannot distinguish one from the other as all become one. What does the wind represent? Some days, it feels more like a whirligig than a pinwheel, when one element might be missing or those times when the whole experience feels out of balance.

B. CAT'S CRADLE: THINKING AND LEADERSHIP

There are situations where thinking and leadership are completely intertwined, like a rope—the rope is collaboration. There are other strands—is that what these are: strands?

Explore metaphors, rope, strands; don't get hung up over it.

> What image comes to your mind? Describe your metaphor using the language of educator collaboration found in the framework.

2 ❧ Professionalism

On occasion I am asked to suggest additions to the curriculum primarily in language arts and social science. As I present any given book title to classroom teachers, I consider the "raising the bar versus dumbing down" issue, and I know which teachers will be concerned about it and in what way. I also want to be sure that I am honoring that element whereby the teacher is focused on the students' needs, expectations, and aspirations. I verbalize that so that teachers can explicitly experience this very professional encounter.

There is an expectation of professionalism which I meet with pleasure by being prepared and sensitive to the circumstances surrounding the encounter. The act of questioning is part of the professional volley.

Why is preparation an important element of professionalism particularly in the context of educator collaboration?

3 ❧ Individuality

A teacher creates an environment wherein she feels good about herself as a model to the students and a partner to the resource educator.

In a recent conversation with a teacher, she told me that she is no longer doing any individual assignment because she has to teach lockstep with her colleagues: "We are on the same page in the textbook on the same day. I can't collaborate because I can't do anything as an individual anymore; I have no individuality." To those who do not act as individuals, they are not missing anything. She is not feeling good about herself as a teacher.

For example, she no longer reads aloud five minutes a day. I asked her why she stopped that practice that she enjoyed so much, and she rapidly explained that five minutes a day is twenty-five minutes a week, etc. . . . and she doesn't have the time because her class would be behind the others. I made a small suggestion that she accepted and felt better, as if I had given her permission to be an individual.

Why do some think that individuality is counterintuitive to collaboration? What is your take on this?

4 ⇜ What Is Success?

The research-topic-type-of-assignment is the bread and butter of the school library program at the moment. It provides the perfect match of teacher and librarian in a collaborative experience. *The success of such an experience lies in the students' achievement in gaining understanding from the assignment as designed by the collaborating educators.* The additional benefit of a student evaluation helps the collaborators fine-tune the assignment for the next go-around.

For collaboration to be effective and, we hope, successful, the students need to be taken into account. Right. The more directly this is approached, the closer the fit of the lesson and the students. Talking to teachers about their students is an intimate conversation. It is akin to talking to someone about her family members. They sense that the students reflect on them as teachers, and, at the same time, they feel protective of them. This sensitivity toward the students needs to be honored and fed during the course of the collaboration. To some teachers, the thought of customizing the curriculum to meet their students' needs and interests is like a dream.

Collaboration has a focus.

How are we adding texture to each other's work?

5 ⚬⚬ Celebrate!

There is an air of celebration about collaboration that one gets from stretching one's mind, taking a deep breath, and looking through fresh eyes. The exaltation comes from sharing this feeling with a kindred professional. Together we rise above the daily realia and find new vistas.

The dance of collaboration is an antidote to the weight of "administrivia" and puts lockstep teaching to the test. It takes the dregs of self-worth left by standards and testing and turns the teacher into an inspired and rejuvenated partner in design.

The reward is richer because it can be shared; it follows from "learning as social interaction." Vygotsky relates to teachers as well as students; all learning is social, not just for children. It also relates to the community of learners à la Brown and Campione. The key is for the teachers to perceive themselves as learners. Once that is accomplished, social learning, community of learners, constructivist teaching principles, and practitioners as researchers are all fair game. There has to be a place in preservice education for this perception to be experienced, taught, and reinforced.

> *Why is celebration an integral part of the collaboration process?*

6 ⚬⚬ Info(rmation) Lit(eracy)

The information literacy curriculum has a unique power to bring educators together to best instruct their students. It benefits from the power of both the classroom teacher and the resource educator. Authentic research, engaged learning, and problem- or project-based learning can all use information literacy as a strategy for research.

The collaborations that result from these experiences are truly balanced because the success of the unit relies on both the content and the strategy applied. This is a perfect blend of practitioner knowledge that directly impacts student learning. Transfer of learning is a key element in each of these designs.

> *What was it about the information literacy curriculum that moves the teacher to initiate a collaborative experience?*

7 ⟡ The Patient Died

The collaborative experience was deep and meaningful, but the students were not engaged—the operation was a success, but the patient died.

According to the discouraged teacher, few students "got it." The unit was too isolated and too different from anything else the students had ever done. A single research paper cannot accomplish all that we had hoped when the students had no prior experiences with this kind of critical thinking or community of learners. There is a building process that is necessary, scaffolding, an atmosphere that encourages deep thinking, an environment that can accommodate students discussing research topics and helping each other.

The richness of the collaboration between the educators is hard to deny, but there is work to be done beforehand to prepare students to attend to a new intellectual task.

How do we ensure that the patient lives?

8 ❧ R-E-S-P-E-C-T – Find Out What It Means to Students

A MEDLEY IN THREE PARTS

A. Do preservice and professional development programs address the issue of respect? I have seen clearly the effect that showing students respect has on them. The lesson is an obvious one, but the question is, Can this critical lesson be taught or is it too late once a person is a college student or a practitioner?

> *How can the genuine respect that some teachers show their students be taught?*

B. "Where the students are."

Some educators just don't get that. They talk about "dumbing down" and "getting back to basics" and "teachers are not their students' parents; schools are not social agencies."

> *How does the acknowledgement of "where the students are" impact collaboration?*

C. The element of RESPECT FOR STUDENTS is strong. As are INDIVIDUALITY and OWNERSHIP. Think about not treating students like second-class citizens, for example.

> *What about that connection between respect for self and respect for others? How does it relate to teachers re: students re: collaboration?*

9 &ᶜᵉ Surprise! Creativity = Ownership/Individuality

By sharing ownership, a teacher saw the individuality that creativity requires and related to the collaborative experience in that way. As a teacher who is comfortable when he works alone, he found something through the process of the collaboration that he valued—his individuality. He was surprised that he did not lose it, that it was strengthened and even highlighted through the process. Then, through experiencing his own creativity, he encouraged his students to be creative and express their individuality. This experience is awash with surprise.

He was surprised and pleased. He said that they did a great job on the posters and some of the students "really got into it."

> *Describe how a heightened sense of individuality adds to creativity. So, who wants creative students?*

10 &ᶜᵉ Time, Time, Time, See What's Become of My Lesson

Time is a factor that impacts oh so many issues for teachers. In some cases, it has a major influence on class management. A teacher finds that time works against him although it is a necessary element of his curriculum design.

The teacher works hard to balance lesson design with the time he is allotted, but the students can be too much for him and put the kibosh on best-laid plans.

> *How do we stay fluid so that the students do not internalize our adult fixation on time and the dire implications of losing it forever?*

11 &ec We > I + Teacher

$$A = I/Me = 6 \qquad B = Teacher = 7 \qquad C = WE = 15$$

$$C > A + B$$

$$WE > I + Teacher$$

I wrote a reflection of a collaborative experience with an English teacher, a new teacher whom I had just met recently. I reviewed the written reflection and counted words. The word WE is greater than the sum of the two collaborators. This is the formula for optimal collaboration. It permeates even the simplest collaborative experience.

Think about a collaborative partner in or out of school.
When do you think "I" and when do you think "WE"?

Do the math.

12 &ec Engaged Learning and Community of Learners

Go to the literature.

Read Ann Brown in McGilly's *Schools for Thought* and her other articles.

Visit the North Central Regional Educational Laboratory (NCREL) website (ncrel.org) and check out the documentation on engaged learning.

The predominant elements in collaboration here are thinking and learning.

How do these elements fit in with community of learners
and engaged learning vis-à-vis the role of the educator?

Is one possible without the other?

Where is the overlap?

Why is the group structure so important here?

13 ɛɕ Individuality → Positives & Negatives → Sensitivity

There is no element other than individuality that seems to be so fraught with both positives AND negatives.

Those teachers who do invest themselves in units inherited from predecessors and put their personal marks on them do feel more enriched and fulfilled by them and do have a more valuable experience with their students. It is just human nature to feel more deeply about something you worked on yourself than something that was given to you. There IS pride in ownership for intellectual property, and that needs to be acknowledged.

> *What is the relationship between positive individuality and sensitivity? Does collaboration benefit from such sensitivity? Does "sensitivity" appear as a theme where "individuality" does not?*

14 ɛɕ -Ownership + -Individuality = Lookin' for Love in All the Wrong Places . . .

Is collaboration possible with NO ownership and NO individuality?

Some projects that get easier for a teacher after the first time or two unfortunately get moved to the newest teacher, and no one is able to learn from prior experiences.

Consider the teacher as a learner with no prior experience... This should impact new teacher assignments. New class assignments for veteran teachers are also relevant but not as much so since the veteran teacher can transfer knowledge from other past experiences.

No ownership, no individuality, no identity. Attempting collaboration would be like looking for love when one does not know oneself.

> *Idea for a remedy, anyone?*

15 &c. We Are Family: Grants Help Us Create Our Family Trees

The goal of most, if not all, non-library research projects in the school library is community. In most cases, the audience is all members of the school learning community. Breaking down the barriers between school and community is a goal worthy of all educators. Writing grants that include community partners has its ups and downs. We are guaranteed to not receive any grant funds if we do not write grant applications for them. Right.

The outcome of successful grant applications, in addition to the funding, is the sense of community in a lifelong learning way. It is like prophets in your own backyard; we honor the learners all around us and share the joy of learning. Without exposure to the "happenings" (programming organized by the school library staff and directed to the entire learning community), it does not seem clear to many students what their goal in school actually is. I do not think that they see many of the adults around them as learners or as members of the (à la Frank Smith) literacy club. Why join? Why seek? *Why cultivate a curious mind?* Why, indeed, when the emphasis is on testing and standards. Even the teachers lose sight of the big picture and not for a lack of looking but because they cannot see it amidst the mountains of paperwork, "administrivia," tests, and standards.

Collaboration plays a primary role in creating these experiences for community to flourish. Shared ownership and multiple perspectives are key to achieve a broad response.

The collaboration starts as an equal partnership that develops beyond the original goals. The fact that the desired outcomes are unrelated (in a direct way) to the curriculum feeds the synergy of the partners.

> *How can we demonstrate to our students the value of cultivating a curious mind?*
>
> *How do you share yourself as a lifelong learner with your students and colleagues?*

16 &c Single but Engaged

When we think of engaged learning, we always think of groups, like cooperative groups. Even though the students have individual responsibilities within the group, we still consider it to be designed as a group activity.

In attempting to personalize assignments, we find students who are on individual paths immersed in "engaged learning" activities. This happens in authentic research, too. The value of the personalization cannot be overlooked.

Is there a connection between teachers who operate as individuals and their desire to design lessons that allow their students to personalize their work? Will a teacher who does not think like an individual aspire to develop curricula that instill individual engagement in their students? Does engaged learning have to be group-oriented?

Consider this: the teacher who thinks like an individual, yet seeks out a collaborator, is operating as an engaged learner. It follows that this is a powerful direction for students. Do not diminish the role of the individual in the group learning process. The group does not minimize the role of the individual; the strength of the group relies on the strength of its members. In any community of learners, each member must be a "learner" in his or her own right.

We found that over the course of a unit (studying individual authors selected by the students) the students became proprietary about their authors. This sense of ownership was encouraging to us as a testament to the students' engagement. Yes, indeed.

What role does independent research play in engaged learning activities?

17 ❧ Committee = Community?

Why do some committees develop into communities and others do not?

How does community differ from this committee? Some committees do not develop a sense of community, but all have the potential. How can this be used in the classroom to develop community? It works in schools by having committees that include members from all levels of employees. The same integration should work in the classroom.

One teacher nicknamed our ad hoc committee to serve underserved students "Possibilities." That made my heart soar.

In our little ad hoc committee the teachers felt wonderful about their involvement and promised continued support. We all shared ownership and respect for our students.

What is the relationship between collaboration and community? Which fosters which?

18 ❧ Add a Dash of Critical Thinking

It seems so simple to add a dash of critical thinking. I don't understand why it isn't more prevalent. It is most easily added to simple assignments—those that are not complicated and do not have many steps. Perhaps it is easier to add depth when there is not a lot of breadth.

Adding components of determining, selecting, and comparing could work on many levels with many assignments. It fits well on Bloom's taxonomy. And it adds a needed component to many of the assignments that are now designed around the Internet that do not include any form of higher thinking skills other than the ability to find a useful website.

It is often the case that the collaborative experience revolves around looking at an assignment through fresh eyes that view critical thinking as a necessary ingredient in any valuable exercise. Oftentimes, the teacher has such a focus and direction related to the content that considering the level of thinking required to accomplish the task is not deemed as high a priority. Cover the content, Plato to NATO; teachers feel constrained and overwhelmed. And it is understandable.

Describe a lesson before and after adding a dash of critical thinking. Which one gives us more food for thought?

19 ☙ Super Modeling

We modeled our reading behavior for the students. We were co-teaching the part of the unit that dealt with independent reading. We were trying to explain to the students that they could not compare with others because the assignment was so personalized based on their authors. In doing this we would compare our reading habits and talk about how different they were, and yet we were both readers and we enjoyed discussing our reading choices with each other. We did not realize that this would have an authenticity benefit for some of the students.

Because there was such an emphasis on the personalizing of this author selection, students felt ownership. They discussed this unit at home. Some students found books by these authors in their homes—or they selected authors that they knew family members had read. Either way, the added authenticity was an unexpected outcome of this assignment. The students then saw family members as models. They shared with us information about their family members who read the authors the students had been assigned.

There was a deep connection with many of the students and their authors. They defended them against attacks by fellow students. Adding value to their authors added value to the work they were accomplishing. If there was a family member connected to the author in some way, attacks from other students could feel more personal.

This attachment to the family member's reading behavior through this assignment was fostered by our modeling our reading behavior. The student was awash with adults in his life who read for pleasure. This is a unique experience for many of our students.

In another lesson with another teacher, the authenticity was based on family members who had served in Vietnam.

Then, during the class, the students continued the collaboration as they shared everything they found and helped each other to find new information together. It was a unique and remarkable moment, and I contend that the success of this exercise was because the material had meaning in the students' lives outside of school.

How can we model this concept of engagement effectively so that students make the connection between school and the rest of their lives?

20 ❧ Veteran Teachers versus Newbies

Curricula that include aspects of authenticity, thinking critically, *and* simplicity are all more easily found in the work of veteran teachers than in the work of new teachers. Right or wrong?

There seems to be some solace in considering all veteran teachers to be on that "plateau" (Gary L. Anderson's research on teacher cycles) that is reached after three short years. I have found that veteran teachers, perhaps as they operate from that plateau, have a talent for simple yet meaningful lessons that force students to think deeply about issues that have relevance in their lives.

There seems to be some solace in considering new teachers to be more attuned to the technology and not afraid of it. I find that where new teachers might use the technology for their own purposes, like grade management, veteran teachers are more flexible and willing to risk more with the new technology.

Veteran teachers reach a comfort level with the content in their domain that new teachers seek.

I find that the "necessary conditions" for educator collaboration to occur are derived from both veteran and new teachers, if perhaps in different realms.

> *So who do you think is more prone to test out*
> *a collaborative partnership?*

21 &ce Authenticity and Respect for Students

Two teachers, two cases, "Both teachers who show tremendous 'respect to students' are determined to keep their classes 'real.' Both also happen to be skilled in technology."

What is the connection between authenticity and respect for students? Well, for those of us who agree with the popular notion of the high school as a holding pen for adolescents, we feel that school has to have relevance to the students' lives outside of school.

Both of these teachers work with students who have after-school jobs and could drop out of school if they chose. There is little support for academics at home. These students are living adult lives except when they are in school and are treated like children and second-class citizens.

The only way to keep the students engaged is to keep it "real." Because these teachers have respect for their students, they heed this message and do what they can to keep their material relevant.

What IS the connection between authenticity and respect for students?

22 ᥥᥥ Professionalism and Time

A collaboration is a journey. Sometimes we stand in the river and teach a lesson that resulted from a collaborative experience, but most of the time we continue to move on, building the collaborative partnership in many subtle ways. In reality, the professional partnership continues to build and is strengthened with each experience. Each experience then acts as a basis for prior knowledge. Collaborators who continue to collaborate comment on the richness and depth of the collaboration after many years (e.g., Glaser and Strauss).

Sometimes it is helpful to have a long-range view of collaborative experiences so that it does not feel like an idea that is not pursued immediately is wasted. Seeds of ideas are planted all the time. Collaborative relationships are built over time. The idea that these prompts that represent isolated assignments are unconnected is not the case. Collaborative experiences begat collaborative experiences. In a sense, they are all cumulative. It is just like the building of a relationship. In the case of educator collaboration, a professional relationship.

How does a collaborative relationship differ from your other professional relationships?

23 &c. Authenticity and Individuality (and Did I Mention Respect for Students, Too?)

OK, already—what's the connection? First of all, what makes one teacher in four seek me out to collaborate on an assignment that appears for all intents and purposes to be a done deal?

So what do we do with it? We tweak it and suddenly it is authentic research and engaged learning, and the students are reacting much differently than in the other classes, where the teachers fed the students the formulaic lesson with no personalization, no room for choice.

What we did was to bring the lesson to where the students are, add choice, and relate it to the real world. The teacher took the first step by coming to me to work on this assignment. What is it that brought him to me? He demonstrated his own sense of professionalism, ownership, and individuality.

Without respect for his students, this teacher would not have worked this hard to ensure that they felt personally attached to their topics.

The pattern that is emerging is that the "respect for students" teachers are all teaching "at-risk" students. I do not find the same quality emerging in the accelerated classes. Is more attention given to the individual in lower-ability-level classes because there is more time (less coverage), or do those students need it more to become engaged in their schoolwork?

Is it both? Or neither? These are teachers who show all students respect. They happen to teach that population of students probably because they enjoy it—get positive feedback, that most magical of psychic rewards, and they are good at it.

> *Are we more rushed with accelerated students, trying to cover more content and assuming that they can balance whatever else comes their way? Do we consider "the whole child" more when we teach the lower-ability student? How does time bend in the classroom depending on the ability level of the students?*

24 &ce Formal versus Informal Collaboration

Formalized collaboration rarely works well. Hargreaves calls it "contrived collegiality" in *Changing Teachers, Changing Times:* "In contrived collegiality, collaboration among teachers was compulsory, not voluntary; bounded and fixed in time and space; implementation—rather than development-oriented; and meant to be predictable rather than unpredictable in its outcomes."

In one case, I worked informally with a teacher, and subsequently another teacher wanted to join us to receive district-sanctioned professional development credit for the collaborative project. This situation illustrates the contrast in a formalized, externally rewarded collaboration contrivance by the staff development program and our own informal collaboration that was chock-full of hard work, determination, surprise, and student engagement.

Prominent themes in this collaboration were respect for students, balance, caring and sensitivity, process, and modeling learning.

In comparing the two cases, I became interested in the external reward of the professional development units as compared to our informal collaboration with no external incentive. We were completely committed to the success of our unit. The experience with the third party made all the more poignant our initial shared internal motivation.

What is an administrator to do? Put yourself in her pumps.

25 Respect for Students—Have I Mentioned This Before??

We have great success with those students who are "at-risk" by providing the Freshman Academy and the Core (Chapter one) programs. What elements from these programs can we transfer to the regular classroom?

We collaborate, we team teach, we have common prep time, we have smaller classes, and we have more adults (instructional assistants) per class. We coordinate language arts and social science. We have established an in-school business that the students operate.

We also celebrate achievements and build in more rituals and public rewards. We plan explicit rites of passage. We involve families.

Take this lesson back to the regular classroom.
What would that look like?

26 Growing Lessons

The growth process for lessons varies. "Sometimes small but important steps work best."

Where there is a balance of leadership with an emphasis on professionalism, preparation, and respect for students, the shaping process is timely. In order for the community of learners to have engaging materials, the collaborating educators have to take a long view of the learning process and allow for a flexible time element.

Where these conditions do not exist and the goal of the lesson is the short term, the students will have a truncated learning experience. What is the point of this mini-lesson? Perhaps the teacher has found that it is functional in giving the students just the essence of the background knowledge that they need to read a novel set in a different country. That is giving the teacher the whopping benefit of the doubt.

Do lessons grow, evolve? Are they dynamic or static?

27 ⟨⟨⟨ Does Every Unit Have a Limit?

". . . but we did not go that far with it." Every unit has a limit, and it is important to know when to stop. That is something that I am continually learning. Most of the teachers I work with have a better sense of that. I am learning . . .

Is that something that I SHOULD learn? Maybe it helps to collaborate with someone who does not know the limits, boundaries, barriers, and borders. Maybe it is more effective to keep an open mind in regard to the limits on single lessons and units.

The one condition that makes the collaborative experience smooth and sustainable is BALANCE.

Throughout the beginning months of our collaboration, this teacher often voiced his concern that he was overstepping his bounds and "using" me too much. I told him that our project was very much a part of my job and that he should enjoy it. He could not understand why everyone doesn't work this way. If everyone did want a collaborative experience along the lines of what we accomplished, it would not be possible. That is why some of the efforts at formal collaboration don't always work out so well. There is something about the irregularity, the intrinsic motivation, the dependence on a professional colleague for voluntary partnership that gets lost when mandates are handed down. I question if a "top-down" collaboration requirement has much chance of working for professionals who are intrinsically motivated.

How are long-term collaborations sustained? What if all partners do not concur that they are "limitless"?

28 ✎ Balance/Leadership/Learning/ Creativity

All of the educators involved in these units have a deep interest in the topic of South Africa. There is a camaraderie based on concern for the people and a fascination with the region's history. How do the students benefit from our deep interest in this topic?

The themes of balance, leadership, learning, and creativity all seem to be interwoven:

We are all very interested in this topic personally, and we converse and engage and enjoy this common bond . . . We feed off of each other's deep interest . . . We learn from each other, and we know that we each have a kindred spirit. There is much professional respect in our relationship as we value each other's interest in this emotionally charged subject.

Why should we model our mutual intellectual curiosity for students?

29 ∽ Preparedness and Creativity

There is a quote I can't place about being ready to be inspired . . . I think that it is in Vera John-Steiner's book *Notebooks of the Mind.* Look it up. Here is another one about the prepared mind:

"Energy and commitment are needed in shaping the inner short-hand of ideas into publically available work—the joining of thought and realization—which is sustained in a variety of ways: by 'the courage to create,' by a well-honed discipline **and a fully-prepared mind,** and by the artist's passion for his or her task" (emphasis added) (p. 79).

I still think that there is another, shorter quote about being prepared to be spontaneous . . .

I do agree that there is a readiness, an attention that needs to be corralled to be creative. In order to deviate you need to know what you are deviating from—to go beyond the curriculum you have to be conversant in the curriculum.

I believe that to be innovative, creative, and inventive in an informed way, you have to start from a solid foundation of preparedness.

"The more solid your foundation the more freedom you have to be inventive in an informed way" (British film director Mike Leigh).

What is the connection between preparedness and creativity?

30 ⤳ Respect for the Students + High Expectations = Chicken or the Egg?

When we show students respect by holding high expectations and they rise to the occasion, what came first, the chicken or the egg? In these cases, we had emotional attachment, authenticity, respect for students, and high expectations. The authenticity comes with respect for students and a desire to connect to the student as a whole person and not just a high school student.

Respect for students includes recognizing the students for who they are and where they have been. Showing respect means placing realistic demands that stretch the student in both his heart and his head. The added dimension of considering adolescent psychology and behavior shows a commitment to students that goes beyond the every day. It does not pander but just seeks to use what we understand to be adolescent behavior.

> *Think about Piaget, Erikson, Kohlberg. Yes, our students may have adult responsibilities, but they are still growing and developing. Chicken or egg?*

31 ᘓᙓᙒ Ownership, Preparation, and Risk

When teachers are willing to risk and to give up control, they must have a sense that the price they are paying will be worthwhile for the benefit of student learning. What is it that gives them this sense? Do they believe in their collaborator and the power of the collaborative experience to produce something valuable, or do they, more basically, believe in themselves and their instincts as teachers?

Ownership issues pervade many collaborative efforts. Preparation also figures prominently. From past experience, each of these teachers knows that I am (try to be) always prepared and that I do not hesitate to ask for more information as needed. They each had faith in me to carry off the performance necessary in these cases, as a storyteller and a guest speaker. All the teachers gave me complete control of their classes.

What were the conditions that caused these three teachers to seek me out for these collaborative experiences? They knew that I had talents that could enhance their students' learning. They knew that I would be prepared and that their ownership issues and loss of control were safe with me. They had seen their students interact with me and knew that I was up to the task. And they were willing to risk the unknown for a little bit of unpredictable results with the hope that the students would benefit from the experience. In each case, the teachers gave up one class period for these performances.

These teachers believed in themselves as teachers, in their individuality in seeking out something that goes beyond the normal boundaries. They trust both themselves and me, and they respect their students enough to go the extra mile with the hope that it will be worthwhile.

The students were transported beyond the school walls into the story world. With their teachers' permission, they went on a journey with me. As with the power of story, their teachers knew that I promised to bring them home safely. We broke down those barriers and created a lasting memory. That is the power of story. These teachers were willing to risk in order for their students to have this experience—one which they could not have had without our collaborative effort.

> *How do we build capacity together that simply cannot be achieved alone? How do our students benefit?*

32 ∽ How Many Educators Does It Take to Change a Lightbulb?

There are things that you can do when you have many hands helping. In two particular cases, there is a low student-to-teacher ratio.

Also, in each of these cases, the "teachers" are a variety of educators: classroom teacher, reading specialist, librarian, bilingual teacher, and teacher's aides. Knowing that there will be so many guides for the students really impacts the lesson you can develop.

The environment is impacted because you can rely on so many facilitators. It makes for a collaborative environment because the more that the "teachers" are working together, the better learning experience the students will have.

> *The question is begged, can you have too much of a good thing?*

33 ∽ Metacognition and Reflection as Habits of Mind?

In some instances, metacognition, self- and group-reflection, and self- and group-evaluations figure prominently. There is a deep concern for the intellectual lives of the students that directs these purposes.

In the one case, I modeled my metacognition as the teacher and I demonstrated argument and counter-argument. It showed our honesty in presenting the material, and it expressed our trust and respect for the maturity of the students.

In two other cases, journals or logs were used as tools for self- and group-reflection.

"This simple tool is very effective as a metacognitive probe to help to develop habits of mind for these young adults." "The group research journal acted as a situated cognition tool that recorded the distributed cognition of the group."

All of the above fit under the theme of "thinking." The natural connections are to learning, teaching, and modeling.

> *Think about how you think and learn.*
> *How does this self-knowledge inform your practice?*

34 &ce; When It's Hot, It's Hot, and When It's Not, It's Hot. What Is It?

Technology adds an entire dimension to some discussions. More than a theme, it has impact over anything it wants—like the 800-pound gorilla.

The collaboration that goes into lessons that include technology is often quite elaborate. Sometimes this may be a result of the teacher's newbie status. The students do not think that it is so elaborate. The teacher, as a computer-as-a-second-language speaker, translates lessons into technology. The students need no translation. Then, because of the unpredictable nature of technology, collaboration continues full-force during each lesson because of the flexibility that is required to handle anything, come what may.

In one such case, technology that was expected to work, the copier, did not, which led to a deepening of the creative aspect of the lesson. Technology that was not expected to enhance the project, a CD-ROM, broadened the scope of the goal of the assignment.

Technology was responsible for enhancing this assignment with two new creative twists. First, technology that did not work added to the creativity by forcing students to draw their plants. Second, technology that was unexpected added the dimensions of growth and blooming. Students added these aspects of the plant to their metaphors . . . These two impromptu collaborative experiences resulted in the students having a richer learning experience (Bush, 2001).

> *We think of technology as expanding our opportunities to enhance learning. Is this always the case?*

35 ཉཉ Once Upon a Time in the Preschool

By seeking out the environment, the collaboration became a natural consequence.

I sought out the preschool, became a part of the structure, and the collaboration followed with no forethought on either of our parts. This collaboration has a story that begins in a completely unintentional way. Seeking out the preschool—like Glass seeking out psychoanalysis studies and ending up developing meta-analysis.

The strength of this bond is that it continued as collaborators changed. Old left, new came, and still the collaborative experience continued and grew deeper.

What conditions were present that initiated the collaboration? Not just personal conditions in this case but environmental ones as well. An atmosphere of partnership was built up over time. The collaboration seemed like a natural progression, like it would have seemed strange for it not to develop. This is not a result of "personalities" as many would like to think about collaboration.

In another case, the new faculty orientation is more blatant in the attempt to establish an environment that is conducive to collaborative experiences. Is that so wrong?

Is there a difference in the student learning as a result of a collaboration that grows out of the learning environment than one that is created for the sake of the lesson?

36 ❧ From the Mouths of Student Teachers

I have been told by a student teacher that she was afraid that collaborating with the librarian would indicate a weakness on her part; she felt that her command of the content matter would be questioned by both her cooperating and her supervising teachers.

This goes along with the student of preservice teachers being influenced more by the cooperating teacher than any strategy learned in teacher education.

This also provides the negative case for the strength of Conversation Prompt 3 on page 97.

I do not think that this is an isolated case. I believe that if student teachers and first-year teachers were surveyed, this would be a prevailing sentiment . . . thanks to teacher education and cooperating teachers.

We do have student teachers who collaborate with other educators. Where does the difference lie? If you are a practitioner, think back. If you are a preservice educator, think ahead.

37 ⊷ Synergy = The Final Frontier

In a mad dash for yet another overused buzzword, *synergy* raises its perky head.

The "students" (teachers in in-services and workshops) that we have always enjoy taking our classes . . . It is clear to us that our energy feeds off of itself, we create a synergy, and together we produce much more than either of us could do alone or with another partner. Our total is far greater than the sum of our parts.

So, we are collaboration personified in a sense. We have collaborated together for so many years in so many different circumstances, our collaboration has taken on a life of its own. There are times when things work out just fine, but the results are not what either of us intended. We delight in being surprised by this, but, then again, nothing surprises us too much when we get cookin'. The unpredictability of the results seems to be predictable. We have learned to "trust our instincts" when we collaborate. We are well aware of how much we continue to learn from each other, how balanced our leadership roles are, and in what ways our creativity can be best expressed.

> *Wow. Describe your own wow, or the closest thing to it. It does not have to come from your professional life.*

38 &cc Community Is to Collaboration–Again

In two cases, it is community that is the goal and the result of the collaborative experiences. In order for community to be realized, there has to be an environment in which it can thrive. Chicken, egg. Collaborative experiences foster community, and community fosters collaboration.

In one case, there is now an environment that was developed over a period of six years. During that time, as a result of this collaboration, countless tendrils were working to permeate this atmosphere throughout the school community (and the nation because of the publication of articles about this project).

In another case, there was a conscious effort to encourage a community of readers to grow at our school. This collaboration is one of joy because it is a natural progression that I started, but others carry forth and find collaboration and texture by sharing the literary pieces that I put into place. The richness that is gained from community efforts within the school cannot be overstated.

The impact on student learning is less direct, but considering all members of the community to be learners, it does impact learners in our school community.

> *Most people like to be included, asked for help, invited to share what they know. Or not? Is there a difference in our personal and professional lives?*

39 ❧ Carpe Diem = Teachable Moment

Bless the young-at-heart, energetic teachers who seize, desire, connect, and who, most of all, know their students.

In one case, the special education teacher has much leverage with her time. She seeks out material that will catch her students, and then she pounces. Some of that zeal may come from teaching special education, but some of it is her conviction that the students need to be invested in the topic for it to matter to them. This can certainly be generalized to many regular education students.

In another case, the teacher sought to connect the students by personalizing the unit to match their cultural backgrounds. She was determined for this unit to matter to her students, and together we made that happen.

In both cases, it was the strong desire to reach their students that brought these teachers to seek out a collaborative experience.

> *How do we teach and/or reinforce that "strong desire to reach students"? Is it a teachable skill or an inherent quality?*

40 &co Committee, Community. You Say Potato . . .

When is a committee not a community? That's an easy one. We have all been on committees that did not feel like communities. We thought about this before in Conversation Prompt 17 on page 107. But what are the conditions that impact the community when the vehicle for the committee is technology?

In one case, this committee hums like a well-oiled community. One of the driving forces is the impact that technology has had on our roles within the schools. We need each other in a more pressing way, and we are ready to learn from each other.

In another case, technology was the vehicle around which the committee was established. This was 1995, and we were members of an online discussion that would culminate in a panel discussion. We had a motivation, but we felt that the technology was an obstacle. These feelings would be different today, now that we regularly have online relationships. The structure of the discussions did give us all a shared frame of reference and a common prior experience. When we did come together for the panel discussion, there were glimmers of community just from having "fought the battle" together. We were made to feel that we had accomplished a pioneering feat. The panel discussion did benefit from the committee online discussions. The collaborative experience was real notwithstanding its virtual roots.

> *Why is community such an overriding theme in education today? Do our schools reflect society, or is it the other way around?*

 *Bibliography*

Abdal-Haqq, I. (1992). Professionalizing teaching: Is there a role for professional development schools? *Eric Digest, 91*(3), 1-4. ED 347 153. [Online]. Available: http://www.ed.gov/databases/ERIC_Digests/ed347153.html [5/28/02].

American Association of School Librarians and Association for Educational Communications and Technology [AASL & AECT]. (1998a). *Information literacy standards for student learning.* Chicago: American Library Association.

American Association of School Librarians and Association for Educational Communications and Technology. (1998b). *Information power: Building partnerships for learning.* Chicago: American Library Association.

American heritage dictionary of the English language (3rd ed.). (1992). Boston: Houghton Mifflin.

Anderson, G.L., & Herr, K. (1999). The new paradigm wars: Is there room for rigorous practitioner knowledge in schools and universities? *Educational Researcher, 28*(5), 12-21, 40.

Anderson, J. (1983). *The architecture of cognition.* Cambridge, Mass.: Harvard University Press.

Armstrong, T. (1998). *Awakening genius in the classroom.* Alexandria, Va.: Association for Supervision and Curriculum Development.

Ayers, W. (1993). *To teach: The journey of a teacher.* New York: Teachers College Press.

Ayers, W., Hunt, J.A., Quinn, T. (Eds.) (1998). *Teaching for social justice: A democracy and education reader.* New York: Teachers College Press.

Banks, J.A. (2000). The social construction of difference and the quest for educational equality. In R.S. Brandt (Ed.), *Education in a new era: 2000 ASCD yearbook* (pp. 21-46). Alexandria, Va.: Association for Supervision and Curriculum Development.

Bean, T.W. (1997). Preservice teachers' selection and use of content area literacy strategies. *The Journal of Educational Research, 90*(3), 154-163.

Bogue, C., & Bush, G. (1999). Come join the Readers' Society: A student-directed book discussion group. *Illinois Reading Council Journal, 27*(1), 8-15.

Bosworth, K., & Hamilton, S.J. (Eds.). (1994). Collaborative learning: Underlying processes and effective techniques. *New Directions for Teaching and Learning, 59.* San Francisco: Jossey-Bass.

Brandt, R.S. (Ed.). (2000). *Education in a new era: 2000 ASCD yearbook.* Alexandria, Va.: Association for Supervision and Curriculum Development.

Bransford, J.D., Brown, A.L., & Cocking, R.R. (Eds.). (2000). *How people learn: Brain, mind, experience, and school.* Washington, D.C.: National Research Council.

Bringuier, J. (1980). *Conversations with Jean Piaget.* (B.M. Gulati, Trans.). Chicago: University of Chicago Press. (Original work published in 1977).

Brooks, J.G., & Brooks, M.G. (1993). *In search of understanding: The case for constructivist classrooms.* Alexandria, Va.: Association for Supervision and Curriculum Development.

Brooks, J.G., & Brooks, M.G. (1999). The courage to be constructivist. *Educational Leadership, 57*(3), 18-24.

Brown, A.L. (1997). Transforming schools into communities of thinking and learning about serious matters. *American Psychologist, 52*(4), 399-413.

Brown, A.L., & Campione, J.C. (1992). Students as researchers and teachers. In J.W. Keefe & H.J. Walberg (Eds.), *Teaching for thinking* (pp. 49-59). Reston, Va.: National Association of Secondary School Principals.

Brown, A.L., & Campione, J.C. (1994). Guided discovery in a community of learners. In K. McGilly (Ed.), *Classroom lessons: Integrating cognitive theory* (pp. 229-270). Cambridge, Mass.: MIT Press.

Bruner, J.S. (1996). *The culture of education.* Cambridge, Mass.: Harvard University Press.

Burnaford, G., Fischer, J., & Hobson, D. (Eds.). (1996). *Teachers doing research: Practical possibilities.* Mahwah, N.J.: Lawrence Erlbaum Associates.

Burnaford, G., Fischer, J., & Hobson, D. (Eds.). (2001). *Teachers doing research: The power of action through inquiry.* Mahwah, N.J.: Lawrence Erlbaum Associates.

Bush, G. (1996). The high-interest collection: A stepping stone to students. *School Library Journal, 42*(10), 44.

Bush, G. (1997a). Let it begin with me: Advocating for youth activism. *Voices of Youth Advocates (VOYA), 20*(4), 229-231.

Bush, G. (1997b). Speak muses (Random acts of poetry). *School Library Journal, 43*(9), 139.

Bush, G. (1998a). Be true to your school: Real-life learning through the library media center. *Knowledge Quest, 26*(3), 28-31.

Bush, G. (1998b). Prophets in your own backyard. *Educational Leadership, 56*(1), 46-49.

Bush, G. (1998c). *Secondary content area teacher education for instructional collaboration: A qualitative study.* Unpublished paper. Loyola University Chicago.

Bush, G. (1999). Creating an information literate school: Here and now. *NASSP Bulletin, 83*(605), 62-67.

Bush, G. (2000). *The principal's manual to your school library media program.* [Brochure]. Chicago: American Association of School Librarians.

Bush, G. (2001). Just sing: Creativity and technology in the library media center. *Knowledge Quest, 30*(2), 11-14.

Bush, G., & Kwielford, M.A. (2001). Marketing reflections: Advocating in action. *Teacher Librarian, 28*(5), 8-12.

Cameron, J. (1992). *The artist's way: A spiritual path to higher creativity.* New York: Putnam.

Checkley, K. (2000). The contemporary principal: New skills for a new age. *Education Update, 42*(3), 1, 4-6, 8.

Clandinin, D.J., & Connelly, F.M. (1996). Teachers' professional knowledge landscapes: Teacher stories—stories of teachers—school stories—stories of schools. *Educational Researcher, 25*(3), 24-30.

Clandinin, D.J., Davies, A., Hogan, P., & Kennard, B. (Eds.). (1993). *Learning to teach, teaching to learn: Stories of collaboration in teacher education.* New York: Teachers College Press.

Clark, C.T., Herter, R.J., & Moss, P.A. (1998). Continuing the dialogue on collaboration. *American Educational Research Journal, 35*(4), 785-791.

Clark, C.T, Moss, P.A., & Goering, S. (1996). Collaboration as dialogue: Teachers and researchers engaged in conversation and professional development. *American Educational Research Journal, 33*(1), 193-231.

Cochran-Smith, M., & Lytle, S.L. (1993). *Inside/outside: Teacher research and knowledge.* New York: Teachers College Press.

Cochran-Smith, M., & Lytle, S.L. (1999). The teacher research movement: A decade later. *Educational Researcher, 28*(7), 15-25.

Cohn, M.M., & Kottkamp, R.B. (1993). *Teachers: The missing voice in education.* Albany: State University of New York Press.

Coleridge, S.T. (1970). *The rime of the ancient mariner.* (G. Doré, Illus.). New York: Dover. (Original work published in 1834).

Conant, J. (1963). *The education of American teachers.* New York: McGraw-Hill.

Confrey, J. (1995). How compatible are radical constructivism, sociocultural approaches, and social constructivism? In L.P. Steffe & J. Gale (Eds.), *Constructivism in education* (pp. 185-225). Hillsdale, N.J.: Lawrence Erlbaum Associates.

Costa, A., & Kallick, B. (Eds.). (2000). *Discovering and exploring habits of mind.* Alexandria, Va.: Association for Supervision and Curriculum Development.

Council for Exceptional Children. (1995). *CEC homepage: Our mission* [Online]. Available: http://www.cec.sped.org/ab/purpose.html [5/28/02].

Council for Exceptional Children [CEC]. (1998). *What every special educator must know* (3rd ed.). Washington, D.C.: Author.

Council of Chief State School Officers. (1992). *INTASC core standards* [Online]. Available: http://www.ccsso.org/intascst.html [5/28/02].

Council of Chief State School Officers. (1996). *Standards for school leaders* [Online]. Available: http://www.ccsso.org/isllc1.html [5/28/02].

Cramer, S.F. (1998). *Collaboration: A success strategy for special educators.* Boston: Allyn and Bacon.

Cruickshank, D.R. (1984). *Models for the preparation of America's teachers.* Bloomington, Ind.: Phi Delta Kappa Educational Foundation.

Cruickshank, D.R. (1996). *Preparing America's teachers.* Bloomington, Ind.: Phi Delta Kappa Educational Foundation.

Csikszentmihalyi, M. (1990). *Flow: The psychology of optimal experience.* New York: HarperPerennial.

Cuban, L. (1990). Reforming again, again, and again. *Educational Researcher, 19*(1), 3-13.

Cuban, L. (1998). *How teachers taught: Constancy and change in American classrooms, 1890-1990* (2nd ed.). New York: Teachers College Press.

Daniels, H., & Bizar, M. (1998). *Methods that matter: Six structures for best practice classrooms.* Portland, Maine: Stenhouse.

Darling-Hammond, L. (1997). *The right to learn: A blueprint for creating schools that work.* San Francisco: Jossey-Bass.

Darling-Hammond, L., Griffin, G., & Wise, A.E. (1992). *Excellence in teacher education: Helping teachers develop learner-centered schools.* Washington, D.C.: National Education Association.

Darling-Hammond, L., Wise, A.E., & Klein, S.P. (1999). *A license to teach: Raising standards for teaching.* San Francisco: Jossey-Bass.

DePree, M. (1992). *Leadership jazz.* New York: Dell.

Dewey, J. (1909). *The school and society.* Chicago: University of Chicago Press.

Dewey, J. (1916). *Democracy and education.* New York: Macmillan.

Dewey, J. (1972). My pedagogic creed. In *The early works, 1828-1898. Volume 5: 1895-98* (pp. 84-95). Carbondale, Ill.: Southern Illinois University Press. (Original work published in 1897).

Duckworth, E. (1997). *Teacher to teacher: Learning from each other.* New York: Teachers College Press.

Education chief cites shortage of "talented, dedicated" teachers. (2000, January 10). *Chicago Tribune*, Section 1, p. 10.

Education Week on the Web. (2000). *Quality Counts 2000* [Online]. Available: http://www.edweek.org/sreports/qc00/ [5/28/02].

Eisner, E.W. (1991). My educational passions. In D.L. Burleson (Ed.), *Reflections: Personal essays by 33 distinguished educators* (pp. 136-145). Bloomington, Ind.: Phi Delta Kappa Educational Foundation.

Elmore, R.F., Peterson, P.L., & McCarthey, S.J. (1996). *Restructuring in the classroom: Teaching, learning, and school organization.* San Francisco: Jossey-Bass.

Erikson Institute. (2000, March). *Handbook for teacher education candidates in the Master of Science in early childhood education degree program.* Chicago: Author.

Evans, R. (1996). *The human side of school change.* San Francisco: Jossey-Bass.

Feiman-Nemser, S., & Floden, R.E. (1986). The cultures of teaching. In M.C. Wittrock (Ed.), *Handbook of research on teaching* (3rd ed., pp. 505-526). New York: Macmillan.

Fessler, R., & Christensen, J.C. (1992). *The teacher career cycle: Understanding and guiding the professional development of teachers.* Boston: Allyn and Bacon.

Fishbaugh, M.S.E. (Ed.). (2000). *The collaboration guide for early career educators.* Baltimore, Md.: Paul H. Brookes.

Fitzpatrick, K.A. (1997). *Indicators of schools of quality: A research-based self-assessment guide for schools committed to continuous improvement: Vol. 1. Schoolwide indicators of quality.* Schaumburg, Ill.: National Study of School Evaluation.

Fitzpatrick, K.A. (1998). *Program evaluation: Library media services.* Schaumburg, Ill.: National Study of School Evaluation.

Flinders, D.J. (1988). Teacher isolation and the new reform. *Journal of Curriculum and Supervision, 4*(1), 17-29.

Fogarty, R. (1999). Architects of the intellect. *Educational Leadership, 57*(3), 76-79.

Freire, P. (1998). *Teachers as cultural workers: Letters to those who dare teach: The edge: Critical studies in educational theory.* (D. Macedo, D. Koike, & A. Oliveira, Trans.). Boulder, Colo.: Westview Press.

Friend, M., & Cook, L. (2000). *Interactions: Collaboration skills for school professionals* (3rd ed.). New York: Addison Wesley Longman.

Fullan, M.G. (1990). Staff development, innovation, and institutional development. In B. Joyce (Ed.), *Changing school culture through staff development: 1990 ASCD yearbook* (pp. 3-25). Alexandria, Va.: Association for Supervision and Curriculum Development.

Fullan, M.G., & Hargreaves, A. (1996). *What's worth fighting for in your school?* (Rev. ed.). New York: Teachers College Press.

Gable, R.A., & Manning, M.L. (1997). The role of teacher collaboration in school reform. *Childhood Education, 73*(4), 219-223.

Gage, N.L. (1993). The obviousness of social and educational research results. In M. Hammersley (Ed.), *Social research: Philosophy, politics and practice* (pp. 226-237). London: Open University and Sage.

Gardner, H. (1999a). *The disciplined mind: What all students should understand.* New York: Simon & Schuster.

Gardner, H. (1999b). *Intelligence reframed: Multiple intelligences for the 21st century.* New York: Basic Books.

Glanz, J. (1998). *Action research: An educational leader's guide to school improvement.* Norwood, Mass.: Christopher-Gordon.

Glaser, B.G. (Ed.). (1995). *Grounded theory: 1984-1994: Volumes I & II.* Mill Valley, Calif.: Sociology Press.

Goodlad, J.I. (1984). *A place called school: Prospects for the future.* New York: McGraw-Hill.

Greene, M. (1988). *The dialectic of freedom.* New York: Teachers College Press.

Grover, R. (1996). *Collaboration: Lessons learned series.* Chicago: American Association of School Librarians.

Hall, E.T. (1976). *Beyond culture.* New York: Doubleday.

Halpern, D.F. (1996). *Thought and knowledge: An introduction to critical thinking* (3rd ed.). Mahwah, N.J.: Lawrence Erlbaum Associates.

Hamilton-Pennell, C., Lance, K.C., Rodney, M.J., & Hainer, E. (2000). Dick and Jane go to the head of the class. *School Library Journal Online* [Online]. Available: http://www.schoollibraryjournal.com/articles/articles/20000401_7475.asp [5/28/02].

Hargreaves, A. (1994). *Changing teachers, changing times: Teachers' work and culture in the postmodern age.* New York: Teachers College Press.

Hart, A.W. (1998). Marshaling forces: Collaboration across educator roles. In Pounder, D.G. (Ed.), *Restructuring schools for collaboration: Promises and pitfalls* (pp. 89-120). Albany: State University of New York Press.

Hayes, C., Grippe, P., & Hall, G.H. (1999). Firmly planted: Building resource teacher program puts roots of professional development into the school building. *Journal of Staff Development, 20*(4), 17-21.

Henderson, J.G. (1996). *Reflective teaching: The study of your constructivist practices* (2nd ed.). Englewood Cliffs, N.J.: Prentice-Hall.

Hirsch, E.D. (1996). *The schools we need and why we don't have them.* New York: Anchor Books.

Hobbs, S.F., Bullough, R.V., Kauchak, D.P., Crow, N.A., & Stokes, D. (1998). Professional development schools: Catalysts for collaboration and change. *The Clearing House, 72*(1), 47-50.

Holmes Group. (1986). *Tomorrow's teachers: A report of the Holmes Group.* East Lansing, Mich.: Author.

Holmes Group. (1990). *Tomorrow's schools: A report of the Holmes Group.* East Lansing, Mich.: Author.

Holmes Group. (1995). *Tomorrow's schools of education: A report of the Holmes Group.* East Lansing, Mich.: Author.

Holmes Partnership. (1998). *Transforming schools and schools of education: A new vision for preparing educators.* Thousand Oaks, Calif.: Corwin Press.

Hubbard, R.S., & Power, B.M. (1993). *The art of classroom inquiry: A handbook for teacher-researchers.* Portsmouth, N.H.: Heinemann.

Hudson, P.J., & Glomb, N.K. (1997). If it takes two to tango, then why not teach both partners to dance? Collaboration instruction for all educators. *Journal of Learning Disabilities, 30,* 442-448.

Illinois State Board of Education [ISBE]. (1998). *Professional development framework* [Online]. Available: http://www.isdc.org/ProfessDevFrmwk.html [5/28/02].

International Reading Association [IRA]. (1998). *Standards for reading professionals: A reference for the preparation of educators in the United States* (Rev. ed.). Newark, N.J.: Author.

Interstate New Teacher Assessment and Support Consortium [INTASC]. (1992). *Model standards for beginning teacher licensing and development: A resource for state dialogue* [Online]. Washington, D.C.: Council of Chief State School Officers. Available: http://www.ccsso.org/intascst.html [5/28/02].

Jackson, P.W. (1968). *Life in classrooms.* New York: Holt, Rinehart.

Jackson, P.W. (1992). *Untaught lessons.* New York: Teachers College Press.

Jersild, A. (1955). *When teachers face themselves.* New York: Teachers College Press.

John-Steiner, V. (1997). *Notebooks of the mind: Explorations of thinking* (2nd ed.). Albuquerque: University of New Mexico Press.

John-Steiner, V. (2000). *Creative Collaboration.* New York: Oxford University Press.

John-Steiner, V., Weber, R.J., & Minnis, M. (1998). The challenge of studying collaboration: Response to C.T. Clark and others. *American Educational Research Journal, 35*(4), 773-783.

Johnson, D.W., Maruyama, G., Johnson, R.T., Nelson, D., & Skon, L. (1981). Effects of cooperative, competitive, and individualistic goal structures on achievement: A meta-analysis. *Psychological Bulletin, 89,* 47-62.

Johnson, L.J., Pugach, M.C., & Devlin, S. (1990). Professional collaboration: Challenges of the next decade. *Teaching Exceptional Children, 22*(2), 9-11.

Kaestle, C. (1993). The awful reputation of educational research. *Educational Researcher, 22*(1), 23-31.

Karpov, Y.V., & Haywood, H.C. (1998). Two ways to elaborate Vygotsky's concept of mediation: Implications for instruction. *American Psychologist, 53*(1), 27-36.

Keating, J., Diaz-Greenberg, R., Baldwin, M., & Thousand, J. (1998). A collaborative action research model for teacher preparation programs. *Journal of Teacher Education, 49*(5), 381-390.

Koerner, J. (1963). *The miseducation of American teachers.* Boston: Houghton Mifflin.

Kouzes, J.M., & Posner, B.Z. (1995). *The leadership challenge: How to keep getting extraordinary things done in organizations.* San Francisco: Jossey-Bass.

Kozol, J. (1991). *Savage inequalities: Children in America's schools.* New York: Harper-Perennial.

Kruse, S.D. (1999). Collaborate. *Journal of Staff Development, 20*(3), 14-16.

Lambert, L. (1995). Leading the conversations. In L. Lambert, D. Walker, D.P. Zimmerman, J.E. Cooper, M.D. Lambert, M.E. Gardner, & P.J.F. Slack (Eds.), *The constructivist leader* (pp. 83-103). New York: Teachers College Press.

Lambert, L., Collay, M., Dietz, M.E., Kent, K., & Richert, A.E. (1997). *Who will save our schools? Teachers as constructivist leaders.* Thousand Oaks, Calif.: Corwin Press.

Lance, K.C. (2000). *LRS (Library Research Service) studies find school libraries make a difference to kids* [Online]. Available: http://www.lrs.org/html/about/school_studies.html [5/28/02].

Lance, K.C., Welborn, L., & Hamilton-Pennell, C. (1993). *The impact of school library media centers on academic achievement.* Castle Rock, Colo.: Hi Willow.

Langer, E.J. (1990). *Mindfulness.* Reading, Mass.: Addison-Wesley.

Langer, E.J. (1997). *The power of mindful learning.* Cambridge, Mass.: Perseus.

Larson, M. (1997). *Making conversation: Collaborating with colleagues for change.* Portsmouth, N.H.: Heinemann.

Leonard, L.J., & Leonard, P.E. (1999). Reculturing for collaboration and leadership. *Journal of Educational Research, 92*(4), 237-242.

Lieberman, A. (1995). Practices that support teacher development. *Phi Delta Kappan, 76,* 591-596.

Lieberman, A., & Miller, L. (2000). Teaching and teaching development: A new synthesis for a new century. In R.S. Brandt (Ed.), *Education in a new era: 2000 ASCD yearbook* (pp. 47-67). Alexandria, Va.: Association for Supervision and Curriculum Development.

Lincoln, Y.S., & Guba, E.G. (1985). *Naturalistic inquiry.* Beverly Hills, Calif.: Sage.

Little, J.W. (1990). The persistence of privacy: Autonomy and initiative in teachers' professional relations. *Teachers College Record, 91*(4), 509-536.

Lortie, D.C. (1975). *Schoolteacher: A sociological study.* Chicago: University of Chicago Press.

McGilly, K. (Ed.). (1994). *Classroom lessons: Integrating cognitive theory.* Cambridge, Mass.: MIT Press.

McNamee, G.D. (2000). *Conceptual framework for Erikson Institute's early childhood teacher education program.* Unpublished manuscript, Erikson Institute, Chicago.

Mann, L. (2000). Finding time to collaborate. *Education Update, 42*(2), 1, 3, 8.

Manzo, K.K. (2000). Study shows rise in test scores tied to school library resources. *Education Week on the Web* [Online]. Available: http://www.educationweek. org/ew/ewstory.cfm?slug=28libe.h19 [5/28/02].

Marlowe, B.A., & Page, M.L. (1998). *Creating and sustaining the constructivist classroom.* Thousand Oaks, Calif.: Corwin Press.

Marshall, M.J., & Barritt, L.S. (1990). Choices made, worlds created: The rhetoric of *AERJ. American Educational Research Journal, 27*(4), 589-609.

Marzano, R.J., Brandt, R.S., Hughes, C.S., Jones, B.F., Presseisen, B.Z., Rankin, S.C., & Suhor, C. (1988). *Dimensions of thinking: A framework for curriculum and instruction.* Alexandria, Va.: Association for Supervision and Curriculum Development.

Mattessich, P.W., & Monsey, B.R. (1992). *Collaboration: What makes it work: A review of research literature on factors influencing successful collaboration.* St. Paul, Minn.: Amherst H. Wilder Foundation.

Meier, D. (1995). *The power of their ideas: Lessons for America from a small school in Harlem.* Boston: Beacon.

Meta-Analysis at 25. Gene V Glass Homepage [Online]. Available: http://glass. ed.asu.edu/gene/papers/meta25.html [5/28/02].

Miller, J.L. (1990). *Creating spaces and finding voices: Teachers collaborating for empowerment.* Albany: State University of New York Press.

Moffett, C.A. (2000). Sustaining change: The answers are blowing in the wind. *Educational Leadership, 57*(7), 35-38.

Morocco, C.C., & Solomon, M.Z. (1999). Revitalizing professional development. In M.Z. Solomon (Ed.), *The diagnostic teacher: Constructing new approaches to professional development* (pp. 247-267). New York: Teachers College Press.

Munby, H., & Russell, T. (1996, April). *Theory follows practice in learning to teach and in research on teaching.* Paper presented at the annual meeting of the American Educational Research Association,

New York, N.Y. [Online]. Available: http://educ.queensu.ca/~russellt/96-1-11.htm [5/28/02].

National Board for Professional Teaching Standards [NBPTS]. (2000a). *2000-2001 guide to national board certification* (No. 999-8013-60-7). Washington, D.C.: Author.

National Board for Professional Teaching Standards. (2000b). *What every teacher should know Q & A: The national board certification process, 2000-2001.* [Brochure]. Washington, D.C.: Author.

National Commission on Teacher Education and Professional Standards. (1966). *The real world of the beginning teacher.* Report of the Nineteenth TEPS Conference. Washington, D.C.: National Education Association.

National Education Association. (1982). *Excellence in our schools: Teacher education: An action plan.* Washington, D.C.: Author.

Noffke, S., & Stevenson, R. (1995). *Educational action research: Becoming practically critical.* New York: Teachers College Press.

O'Shea, D.J., & O'Shea, L.J. (1997). Collaboration and school reform: A twenty-first-century perspective. *Journal of Learning Disabilities, 30*(4), 449-462.

Patrick, D. (1999). The role of collaboration in teacher preparation to meet the needs of diversity. *Education, 119*(3), 388-399.

Paul, R. (1993). *Critical thinking: How to prepare students for a rapidly changing world.* Santa Rosa, Calif.: The Foundation for Critical Thinking.

Peck, R.F., & Tucker, J.A. (1973). Research on teacher education. In R.M.W. Travers (Ed.), *Second handbook of research on teaching* (2nd ed., pp. 940-978). Chicago: Rand McNally.

Perkins, D. (1999). The many faces of constructivism. *Educational Leadership, 57*(3), 6-11.

Phillips, J.C. (2000, April). *Beyond drawing boundaries and choosing sides: Why educational leaders need to learn to collaborate.* Paper presented at the American Educational Research Association, New Orleans, La.

Pintrich, P.R. (1994). Continuities and discontinuities: Future directions for research in educational psychology. *Educational Psychologist, 29*(3), 137-148.

Postman, N. (1995). *The end of education: Redefining the value of school.* New York: Random House.

Pounder, D.G. (Ed.). (1998). *Restructuring schools for collaboration: Promises and pitfalls.* Albany: State University of New York Press.

Pugach, M.C., & Johnson, L.J. (2002). *Collaborative practitioners, collaborative schools.* (2nd ed.). Denver: Love.

Purcell-Gates, V. (2000). American Educational Research Association 2001 annual meeting call for proposals. *Educational Researcher, 29*(4), 27-38.

Richardson, V. (1994). Teacher inquiry as professional staff development. In S. Hollingsworth & H. Sockett (Eds.), *Teacher research and educational reform: Part I. Ninety-third yearbook of the National Society for the Study of Education* (pp. 184-199). Chicago: University of Chicago Press.

Rogoff, B. (1990). *Apprenticeship in thinking: Cognitive development in social contexts.* New York: Oxford University Press.

Rogoff, B., & Lave, J. (Eds.). (1984). *Everyday cognition: Its development in social context.* Cambridge, Mass.: Harvard University Press.

Rosenholtz, S.J. (1989). *Teachers' workplace: The social organization of schools.* New York: Longman.

Routman, R. (2002). Teacher talk. *Educational Leadership, 59*(6), 32-35.

Rubin, H. (1998). *Collaboration skills for educators and nonprofit leaders.* Chicago: Lyceum.

Rubin, H. (2002). *Collaborative leadership: Developing effective alliances between communities and schools.* Thousand Oaks, Calif.: Corwin Press.

Sarason, S.B. (1966). *Psychology in community settings: Clinical, educational, vocational, social aspects.* New York: Wiley.

Sarason, S.B. (1971). *The culture of the school and the problem of change.* Boston: Allyn and Bacon.

Sarason, S.B. (1995). Experience in and outside of school. In S.B. Sarason, *School change: The personal development of a point of view* (pp. 196-213). New York: Teachers College Press. (Chapter originally published 1983).

Schön, D.A. (1987). *Educating the reflective practitioner.* San Francisco: Jossey-Bass.

Schrage, M. (1990). *Shared minds: The new technologies of collaboration.* New York: Random House.

Senge, P.M. (1990). *The fifth discipline: The art and practice of the learning organization.* New York: Bantam.

Senge, P.M., Cambron-McCabe, N., Lucas, T., Smith, B., Dutton, J., & Kleiner, A. (2000). *Schools that learn: A fifth discipline fieldbook for educators, parents, and everyone who cares about education.* New York: Doubleday.

Senge, P.M., Kleiner, A., Roberts, C., Ross, R.B., & Smith, B.J. (1994). *The fifth discipline fieldbook: Strategies and tools for building a learning organization.* New York: Doubleday.

Shakespeare, W. (1980). *The first part of the history of Henry IV.* Cambridge: Cambridge University Press. (Original work published in 1597).

Sheridan, S.M. (1992). What do we mean when we say "Collaboration"? *Journal of Educational and Psychological Consultation, 3*(1), 89-92.

Sinaiko, H.L. (1998). *Reclaiming the canon: Essays on philosophy, poetry, and history.* New Haven, Conn.: Yale University Press.

Sizer, T.R. (1984). *Horace's compromise: The dilemma of the American high school.* Boston: Houghton Mifflin.

Sizer, T.R. (1996). *Horace's hope: What works for the American high school.* Boston: Houghton Mifflin.

Sizer, T.R. (1997). *Horace's school: Redesigning the American high school.* Boston: Houghton Mifflin.

Slavin, R.E. (1990). *Cooperative learning: Theory, research, and practice.* Boston: Allyn and Bacon.

Smith, S.C., & Scott, J.J. (1990). *The collaborative school: A work environment for effective instruction.* Eugene, Ore.: ERIC Clearinghouse on Educational Management.

Sparks, D., & Hirsh, S. (1997). *A new vision for staff development.* Alexandria, Va.: Association for Supervision and Curriculum Development.

Sroufe, G.E. (1997). Improving the "awful reputation" of educational research. *Educational Researcher, 26*(7), 26-28.

States lag in skilled teachers, report says. (2000, January 13). *Chicago Tribune.* Section 1, p. 20.

Steffe, L.P. & Gale, J. (Eds.). (1995). *Constructivism in education.* Hillsdale, N.J.: Lawrence Erlbaum Associates.

Bibliography

Steinberg, L. (1996). *Beyond the classroom: Why school reform has failed and what parents need to do.* New York: Touchstone.

Sternberg, R.J. (1997). *Thinking styles.* Cambridge: Cambridge University Press.

Stigler, J.W., & Hiebert, J. (1999). *The teaching gap: Best ideas from the world's teachers for improving education in the classroom.* New York: Free Press.

Strauss, A.L., & Corbin, J.M. (Eds.). (1997). *Grounded theory in practice: A collection of readings.* Thousand Oaks, Calif.: Sage.

Tafel, L.S., & Fischer, J.C. (1996). Lives of inquiry: Communities of learning and caring. In G. Burnaford, J. Fischer, & D. Hobson (Eds.), *Teachers doing research: Practical possibilities* (pp.125-136). Mahwah, N.J.: Lawrence Erlbaum Associates.

Taylor, V.S., Thompson, K., & Schmuck, R.A. (1989). Cross-organizational collaboration: A study of staff development and school improvement efforts in Oregon. *Journal of Staff Development, 10*(2), 16-20.

Thornton, L.J., & McEntee, M.E. (1995). Learner centered schools as a mindset, and the connection between mindfulness and multiculturalism. *Theory into Practice, 34*(4), 250-257.

Tishman, S., Perkins, D.J., & Jay, E. (1995). *The thinking classroom: Learning and teaching in a culture of thinking.* Boston: Allyn and Bacon.

Toffler, A. (1970). *Future shock.* New York: Random House.

Tomkins, J. (1996). *A life in school: What the teacher learned.* Reading, Mass.: Addison-Wesley.

Tudge, J. (1990). Vygotsky, the zone of proximal development, and peer collaboration: Implications for classroom practice.

In L.C. Moll (Ed.), *Vygotsky and education: Instructional implications and applications of sociohistorical psychology* (pp. 155-175). Cambridge: Cambridge University Press.

Tulbert, B. (2000). Practitioners' perspectives of collaboration: A social validation and factor analysis. *Journal of Educational and Psychological Consultation, 11*(3), 357-378.

University of Utah (1998). *Collaboration Telecourse: Prep 1.* (Cassette Recording No. H029K60149). Washington, D.C.: U.S. Department of Education.

Vygotsky, L. (1962). *Thought and language.* Cambridge, Mass.: MIT Press.

Vygotsky, L. (1978). *Mind in society: The development of higher psychological processes.* (Cole, M., John-Steiner, V., Scribner, S., & Souberman, E., Eds.). Cambridge, Mass.: Harvard University Press.

Wald, P.J., & Castleberry, M.S. (2000). *Educators as learners: Creating a professional learning community in your school.* Alexandria, Va.: Association for Supervision and Curriculum Development.

Waller, W. (1932). *The sociology of teaching.* New York: Wiley.

Welch, M. (1998). Collaboration: Staying on the bandwagon. *Journal of Teacher Education 49,* 26-37.

Welch, M. (2000). [Chapter 1 on an eco-systems perspective of collaboration in education]. Unpublished draft.

Wertsch, J.V., & Toma, C. (1995). Discourse and learning in the classroom: A sociocultural approach. In L.P. Steffe & J. Gale (Eds.), *Constructivism in education* (pp. 159-174). Hillsdale, N.J.: Lawrence Erlbaum Associates.

Whitehead, A.N. (1933). *Adventures of ideas.* New York: Macmillan.

Wilson, P.J., & Blake, M. (1993). The missing piece: A school library media center component in principal-preparation programs. *Record in Educational Administration and Supervision, 12,* 65-68.

Windschitl, M. (1999). The challenges of sustaining a constructivist classroom culture. *Phi Delta Kappan, 80*(10), 751-755.

Winer, M., & Ray, K. (1994). *Collaboration handbook: Creating, sustaining, and enjoying the journey.* St. Paul, Minn.: Amherst H. Wilder Foundation.

Winitzky, N., Sheridan, S., Crow, N., Welch, M., & Kennedy, C. (1995). Interdisciplinary collaboration: Variations on a theme. *Journal of Teacher Education, 46*(2), 109-119.

Wise, A.E. (1998). "Assuring quality for the nation's teachers." Testimony at the U.S. Senate Committee on Labor and Human Resources, *Better Teachers for Today's Classroom: How to Make It Happen.* 105th Cong., 2nd session, May 7, 1998.

Wood, D. (1988). *How children think and learn.* Cambridge, Mass.: Blackwell.

Zeichner, K. (1999). The new scholarship in teacher education. *Educational Researcher, 28*(9), 4-15.

Zeichner, K., Melnick, S., & Gomez, M.L. (Eds.). (1996). *Currents of reform in preservice teacher education.* New York: Teachers College Press.

Zemelman, S., Daniels, H., & Hyde, A. (1998). *Best practice: New standards for teaching and learning in America's schools.* (2nd ed.). Portsmouth, N.H.: Heinemann.

 *Index*

Page references to comments from administrators, policymakers, practitioners, and teacher educators print in italic.

A

AASL. *See* American Association of School Librarians (AASL)
Abdal-Haqq, I., 27
accountability
    as impetus for collaboration, 81
    and standards, 83
    transition from control, 55
accreditation of teacher education programs, 29
action as teacher, 70
action research. *See* Teacher/practitioner research
active learners, 44
administrators. *See also* Principals
    as part of learning community, xi
    perspectives on collaboration, 92–93
    role in teacher development, 87
    as users of *Framework*, 83
adolescent psychology (conversation prompt), 118
adult learning, trends in, 33
AECT. *See* Association for Educational Communications and Technology (AECT)
agency in communities of learners, 43
American Association of School Librarians (AASL)
    Information Power, x–xi
    standards, 30, 72, 87
Anderson, Gary L., & Herr, K., 47, 51

applying in constructivism, 44
apprenticeship in social learning, 41
appropriate thinking, 64–65, 66
Armstrong, Thomas, 5
art of teaching, 56
arts, collaboration in, 4
Association for Educational Communications and Technology (AECT)
    Information Power, x–xi
    standards, 30, 72, 87
Association for Supervision and Curriculum Development, 39, 91–92
atmosphere of school, *28*
attitude, 66, *93*
attributes, lists of, 65
authenticity (conversation prompt), 108, 110, 112
autonomy, *26*
    in culture of teaching, 19, 24
    and professional fulfillment, 23
Ayers, William
    mystery of teaching, 25
    school reform, 68–70
    teaching and autobiography, 5–6

B

background of participants
    and implementation of collaboration, 18
    value of knowing, vii
balance in leadership, conversation prompt, 115, 116
    in *Framework*, 75, 81
Banks, J.A., 34
Baratz, Daphna, ix

Bean, T. W., 26
behaviors of collaboration, *14*
bilingual education
    effect of changes on teaching, 34
    need for, 35
bilingual resource teacher, 92
Bohr, Niels, 4
boredom
    students, 44
    teachers, 23
brainstorming
    and conversation prompts, 95
    and creative thinking, 65
    as habit of mind, 39
Brandt, R. S., 34
Braque, Georges, 4
Brooks, J.G., & Brooks, M.G.
    classrooms, 44
    constructivism, 4, 16, 45–46
Brooks, M.G. *See* Brooks, J.G.
Brown, A.L., 43
Brown, A.L., & Campione, J.C., 41, 42–43
BRT (Building Resource Teacher), 54. *See also* Resource educators
Bruner, Jerome S.
    in communities of learners, 43
    definition of collaboration, 3
    vs. Piaget, 40
Building Resource Teacher (BRT), 54. *See also* Resource educators
Burnaford, G., Fischer, J.C., & Hobson, D., x
Bush, G., 7
Bush, G., & Kwielford, M.A., 7
business, collaboration in, 4, 15

C

Cameron, J., 7
Campione, J.C. *See* Brown, A.L.
caring relationships in teacher
    research, 49
Carnegie Task Force on
    Teaching as a Profession, 27
cartography of knowledge, 33
Castleberry, M.S. *See* Wald, P.J.
categories, creation of
    and mindfulness, 60
    and new information, 61
celebration (conversation
    prompt), 99
centers of inquiry, 46
change, *13*, 61, *79*
Chapter one program, 114
Checkley, K., 92
Clandinin, D.J., & Connelly,
    F.M., 53
Clandinin, D.J., Davies, A.,
    Hogan, P., & Kennard, B.,
    28–29
Clark, C.T., Moss, P.A., &
    Goering, S., 10–11
classroom management
    affecting collaboration, 78, 82
    as function of teaching, 27
classrooms, 44
closure methods as metacogni-
    tion skill, 59
Coalition of Essential Schools,
    64, 87
Cochran-Smith, M., & Lytle, S.L.
    criticism of teacher research,
        51
    professional development, x
    standards movement, 48
cognition *vs.* metacognition, 59
Cohn, M.M., & Kottkamp, R.B.,
    51
collaboration, *26*
    comfortable, 14
    communication, 15
    criticisms of, 11–15
    definitions, 2–4
collaborative learning by teach-
    ers, 5–6
collaborative learning environ-
    ment, 11
collaborative lesson planning,
    53
collaborative partners, *59*
    benefits of, 83

unpredictability of partner-
    ships, 76, 79, 82–83
collaborative process, 4
collaborative relationships. *See
    also* Relationships
    partners in, 69
    as sign of weakness, 20
collegiality, contrived
    conversation prompt, 113
    risk of, 37–38
    working against collabora-
        tion, 12–14
comfort levels, *55*
committee work (conversation
    prompt), 107, 127
common or shared language
    development of, 89
    for discussion of collabora-
        tion, 72
    in *Framework*, 71
    and habits of mind, 68
    and metacognition, 58
    and multiple perspectives, 61
communities of scholar-teachers,
    50–52
community as supportive envi-
    ronment, 77, 81–82
community building, *49,* 107,
    125, 127 (conversation
    prompts)
community of learners
    in classrooms, 42
    conversation prompt, 103
competition, *86*
compromise *vs.* collaboration,
    76
Conant, J., 26, 28
Confrey, J., 45
Connecticut State Board of
    Education, 31
connections and patterns, iden-
    tifying, 65
Connelly, F.M. *See* Clandinin,
    D.J.
constructivism
    collaboration in, 11
    and job-embedded learning,
        53
    and leadership, 16
    theory of, 4–6, 43–46
content of instruction, 25, *90. See
    also* Knowledge base
continuing education. *See*
    Professional development

control, 55, *63*
conversation
    as beginning of collabora-
        tion, 92
    leadership of, 45
conversation prompts, 95–127
    uses of, 8, 95
Cook, L. *See* Friend, M.
cooperating teachers
    conversation prompt, 123
    and preservice educators, 26
cooperation *vs.* collaboration, 76
cooperative learning strategy
    adoption of, 44
    and social learning, 41–42
    and teachers as learners, 90
cooperative relationships *vs.* col-
    laboration, 15
coordinated efforts vs collabora-
    tion, 15
coordination *vs.* collaboration,
    76
Core (Chapter one) program,
    114
core concept, collaboration as,
    34
core thinking skills, 39
Costa, Art, 67
Council for Exceptional
    Children (CEC), 31, 35, 72,
    87
Cramer, S.F.
    collaborative learning envi-
        ronment, 11
    special education, 10, 35
creative learners, 44
creative thinking, 64–66, 68
creativity
    and collaborative process,
        6–8, *79*
    conversation prompt, 102,
        117
    in school cultures, 38
Crick, Francis, 4
critical friends groups, 64
critical thinking (directed think-
    ing)
    in collaborative mind-set,
        62–64
    conversation prompt, 107
    as dimension of thinking, 39
    as habit of mind, 67–68
    and loosening of academic
        standards, 33

criticism, fear of, 24
Cruickshank, D.R.
    decision making, 27
    teacher education, 26, 28
Csikszentmihalyi, Mihaly
    creativity, 64
    theory of flow, 43
Cuban, L., 24, 88
culture and social learning, 45
culture of teaching, 19–25, *41, 56, 72*
    changes to, 17, 51
    in communities of learners, 43
    culture of inquiry, 52
    as obstacle, 15, 18, 37–38, 48–50, 68–69
    and school reform, 92

D
Daniels, H. *See* Zemelman, S.
Darling-Hammond, L., Griffin, G., & Wise, A.E., 27, 29
Darling-Hammond, L., Wise, A.E., & Klein, S.P. *See* Interstate New Teacher Assessment and Support Consortium (INTASC)
Darling-Hammond, Linda
    professional development schools movement, 54
    requirements for collaborating teachers, 29
    school reform, 88, 90
Davies, A. *See* Clandinin, D.J.
debriefing as metacognition skill, 59
decision-making
    collaboration as, 4
    as function of teaching, 27
    in process of staff development, 52
democracy
    and public education, 32
    and social justice, 70
demographic trends, 33
DePree, Max, 6, 16
Devlin, S. *See* Johnson, L.J.
Dewey, John
    community of learners, 42
    contributions to constructivism, 45
    process of education, 8
Diamond, Marian, 45

differences in relationships, *21, 43*
differentiated instruction, 45
disabled people, 35
discovery learning, 42, 91
diversity education, 29
Duckworth, E.
    discomfort of collaboration, 16
    professional development, x
DuFour, Rick, 93

E
economic trends, 33
educational research, 47–56
    and policy making, 88
    reputation of, 49
"egg crate schools," 20
Einstein, Albert, 4
Elmore, R.F., Peterson, P.L., & McCarthey. S.J.
    planning time, 86
    reflective process, 16
empowerment, *10*
    results of lack of, 23
    of teachers, 92
energy, *76*
engaged learning (conversation prompt), 106, 108
engagement with others, *50*
enthusiasm, *61*
environment. *See also* Culture of teaching
    nonsupportive, *79*
    in successful collaboration, 15
equality in education, 34
equity in collaboration, *77*
evaluation materials, 43
evaluation of teacher research, 50–51
experimentation in constructivism, 45

F
facilitation as function of teaching, 27
facilitators, outside
    conversation prompt, 120
    in professional development, 56
failure, culture of, *39*
failures, discussion of, 48–49. *See also* Weakness
fashions in theories, 66

feedback as habit of mind, 39
Feiman-Nemser, S., & Floden, R.E., 22
Feuerstein, Reuven, 45
Fischer, J.C. *See* Burnaford, G.; Tafel, L.S.
Floden, R.E. *See* Feiman-Nemser, S.
flow, *78, 83*
Fogarty, R., 44–45
following. *See* Balance in leadership
formality in joint efforts, 15
Fostering Communities of Learners, 43
Framework of Educator Collaboration, 71–84
    purpose of, 8
    use of, 71–72, 81–84
Freire, P., 39
Freshman Academy, 114
Friend, M., & Cook, L
    collaborative ethic, 4
    on collaborative learning environment, 11
frontal teaching, *69*
Fullan, M.G., 52–53
Fullan, M.G., & Hargreaves, A.
    group-imposed boundaries, 13–14
    reflective process, 16–17

G
Gable, R.A., & Manning, M.L., 35
Gage, N.L., ix–x
Gale, J. *See* Steffe, L.P.
Gardner, Howard
    change, 38
    communal nature of teaching, 2
    constructivism, 45
    creativity, 64
    thinking, 39
    trends in public education, 32–33
GDCL (guided discovery in a community of learners), 42–43
gender differences in school culture, 20
general education programs
    standards, 72
    training for, 10

Gilbert, William, 4
Glanz, J., 50
Glaser, Barney G., 3
Glomb, N.K. *See* Hudson, P.J.
goal-oriented collaboration. *See also* Mission in joint efforts
   in *Framework,* 83
   and leadership, 16
goals, *69*
   in creative thinking, 65
   in critical thinking, 62–63
Goering, S. *See* Clark, C.T.
Goodlad, John
   culture of teaching, 21–22
   teacher isolation, 48
   teachers' habits and belief systems, viii
grant writing (conversation prompt), 105
Greene, Maxine, 17
Griffin, G. *See* Darling-Hammond, L.
Grippe, P. *See* Hayes, C.
Grossman, Marcel, 4
group dialogue
   giving sense of freedom, 16
   in teacher research, 50
group-imposed boundaries, 14
group membership in successful collaboration, 15
group work, 42
Gruber, Howard, 7
Guba, E.G. *See* Lincoln, Y.S.
guidance counselors, 92
guided discovery, 42–43
guided instruction *vs.* discovery learning, 91
guided participation in social learning, 41

H

habits of mind
   conversation prompt, 120
   and thinking skills, 39, 66–68
Hall, Edward T., 2
Hall, G.H. *See* Hayes, C.
Halpern, Diane F.
   critical thinking, 62–63
   metacognition, 39
Hammerstein, Oscar, 4
Hargreaves, A. *See also* Fullan, M.G.
   change, 37–38

criticisms of collaboration, 12–13
Hart, A. W., 10
Hayes, C., Grippe, P., & Hall, G. H., 54
Haywood, H.C. *See* Karpov, Y.V.
Heisenberg, Werner, 4
Henderson, J.G.
   centers of inquiry, 46
   teacher research, 50
Herr, K. *See* Anderson, G.L.
Hiebert, J. *See* Stigler, J.W.
Hirsch, E. D., 90–91
Hirsh, S. *See* Sparks, D.
Hobbs, S.F. et al., 10, 54
Hobson, D. *See* Burnaford, G.
Hogan, P. *See* Clandinin, D.J.
holistic environment, 77, *79*
Holmes Group, 6, 27
Holmes Partnership, 6
"Horace Smith" (fictional teacher), 22, 87
Hubbard, R.S., & Power, B.M.
   how-to for teacher research, 50
   shop talk, 49
Hudson, P.J., & Glomb, N.K., 10, 35
Hyde, A. *See* Zemelman, S.

I

idea generation checklist, 65
Illinois State Board of Education, 31
individualism, 2, *86*
   in American history, 4
   in culture of teaching, 20, 24, 38
   and professional identity, 81
   transition to professional community, 55
individuality
   conversation prompt, 97, 102, 104, 112
   in *Framework,* 75
informal collaboration (conversation prompt), 113
information literacy (conversation prompt), 99
information technology
   conversation prompt, 121
   influence of, x–xi
innovation and collaborative process, 6

inquiry
   in constructivism, 45
   culture of, 52
   by preservice educators, 48
   transition from technical work, 55
inquiry, centers of
   and action research, 51
   products of, 46
insider research. *See* Teacher/practitioner research
instructional technology specialists, 92
INTASC. *See* Interstate New Teacher Assessment and Support Consortium (INTASC)
intelligence *vs.* mindfulness, 60
interactive settings in constructivism, 45
interdisciplinary approaches, 33, *51*
International Reading Association (IRA), 72, 87
Internet, 34
interpersonal communication, 23
Interstate New Teacher Assessment and Support Consortium (INTASC)
   collaboration in, 72
   core of knowledge in, 30
   standards, 87
investigation in constructivism, 45
IRA (International Reading Association), 72, 87
isolation of teachers
   in culture of teaching, 14, 19
   effect of technology, 34
   factors contributing to, 21
   and individuality, 81
   paradox of, 22–23
   Rosenholtz on, 11–12

J

Jackson, P.W., 20
Japan, 89–90
Jay, E. *See* Tishman, S.
Jersild, A., 5
job-embedded learning, 53
Jobs, Steven, 4

John-Steiner, Vera
  on Clark, 11
  collaboration in science, 4
  creativity, 7, 38
  criticisms of collaboration,
    14–15
Johnson, L.J., Pugach, M.C., &
    Devlin, S., 35. *See also*
    Pugach, M.C.
journal writing
  and conversation prompts, 95
  job-embedded learning, 53
  and metacognition skills, 59
jugyou kenkyuu (lesson study),
    89–90, 91

K
Kaestle, C., 88
Karpov, Y.V., & Haywood, H.C.,
    42
Kennard, B. *See* Clandinin, D.J.
Klein, S.P. *See* Darling-
    Hammond, L.
knowledge base. *See also*
    Content of instruction
  as dimension of thinking, 39
  existence of, 44
  and multiple perspectives, 61
  as obstacle to teacher
    research, 49
  strengthening of, 55
Koerner, J., 26
Kottkamp, R.B. *See* Cohn, M.M.
Kouzes, J.M., & Posner, B.Z., 15
Kozol, J., 34
Kwielford, M.A. *See* Bush, G.

L
Lambert, L., 45
Lambert, L. et al.
  professional development, x
  reflective process, 16
Langer, Ellen J., 60
Larson, M., 17
Lave, J. *See* Rogoff, B.
"layering" assignments, *24*
Lazarsfeld, Paul F., ix
leadership, *5, 12, 16, 75. See also*
    Balance in leadership
  in classrooms, 24
  in collaborative models,
    15–17
  in constructivism, 45
  in *Framework,* 75

transition from managed
    work, 55
learner-centered instruction
  and collaborative mind-set,
    58
  in constructivism, 45
  and teacher education, 27–28
  vs. teacher-centered instruc-
    tion, 44
learner roles, 44
learning environment (conver-
    sation prompt), 122
learning process
  in constructivism, 43–44
  knowledge as constructed
    entity, 4
  and metacognition, 59
  and social learning, 40–41
learning strategies for collabora-
    tive process, 79
Leonard, L.J., & Leonard, P.E.,
    15
Leonard, P.E. *See* Leonard, L.J.
lesson planning (conversation
    prompt), 114
lesson study, 89–90, 91
librarian-teacher collaboration,
    viii
Lieberman, A., 52
Lieberman. A., & Miller, L.,
    54–55
life lessons, 69–70
lifelong learning (conversation
    prompt), 105
limited English proficiency, 34
Lincoln, Y.S., & Guba, E.G., 51
literacy, functional, 33
Little, J.W.
  criticisms of collaboration, 12
  improvement of teaching, 90
  traditions of teaching, 23–24
long-term professional study
  conversation prompt, 115
  staff development activities
    in, 52
long-term view (conversation
    prompt), 111, 114
Lortie, Dan
  culture of teaching, 20–21
  teacher isolation, 48
  teachers' habits and belief
    systems, viii
Lytle, S.L. *See* Cochran-Smith,
    M.

M
Maine East High School, 35
managed work, 55
Manning, M.L. *See* Gable, R.A.
marginalization of minority
    groups, 33, 34–35
Marlowe, B.A., & Page, M.L., 5,
    43–44
Marzano, R.J. et al., 39
McCarthey. S.J. *See* Elmore, R.F.
McEntee, M.E. *See* Thornton, L.J.
measurement, *88. See also*
    Evaluation of teacher
    research
media, influence of, 33
mediation in constructivism, 45
medical school programs *vs.*
    teacher education, 20, 54
Meier, Deborah
  public education, 32
  school reform, 87
mental management, 39
mentoring programs, 23
metacognition
  in collaborative mind-set,
    58–59
  conversation prompt, 120
  as dimension of thinking, 39
  as habit of mind, 67
  reflection on, 45
  wrapping up, 59
metacognitive mediation, 42
metaphors
  conversation prompt, 96
  as thinking strategy, 65
Miller, J.L., 16
Miller, L. *See* Lieberman. A.
mind-set, collaborative, 4, 57–70
mindfulness
  as consciousness, 59–62
  as habit of mind, 67
Minnesota Board of Teaching, 29
Minnis, Michele, 11
Mischel, Harriet Nerlove, &
    Mischel, Walter, ix
mission in joint efforts, 15. *See
    also* Goal-oriented collabo-
    ration
modeling (conversation
    prompt), 108, 116, 120
Moffett, C.A., 56
Morocco, C.C., & Solomon,
    M.Z., 47–48
Moss, P.A. *See* Clark, C.T.

multiculturalism, 33, 34
Munby, H., & Russell, T., 29
musicians as model of collaboration, 6, 16
mystery of teaching, 25

N

narrative inquiry, 28–29
National Board for Professional Teaching Standards (NBPTS), 30, 85, 87
National Center for Restructuring Education, Schools, and Teaching, 87
National Commission on Excellence in Education, 26–27
National Commission on Teacher Education and Professional Standards, 20
National Education Association, 27
National Study of School Evaluation, 43
"natural" teachers, 2
NBPTS (National Board for Professional Teaching Standards), 30, 85, 87
NCREL (North Central Regional Educational Laboratory), 103
NCREST (National Center for Restructuring Education, Schools, and Teaching), 87
networking in teacher research, 49
Noffke, S., & Stevenson, R., 50
North Central Regional Educational Laboratory (NCREL), 103
NSSE (National Study of School Evaluation), 43

O

occupational socialization. *See* Culture of teaching
off-task conversation, 64
openness to new information, 60–61
optimal experience, 42–43
organizational dynamics
    in successful collaboration, 15
    and teacher-centered instruction, 24

orientation in approach to innovation, 66
originality in creative thinking, 66
O'Shea, D.J., & O'Shea, L.J., 10
O'Shea, L.J. *See* O'Shea, D.J.
outcomes, *81*, 82–83
ownership
    conversation prompt, 102, 104, 119
    teaching profession lacking in, 22

P

Page, M.L. *See* Marlowe, B.A.
Patrick, D., 11
Paul, Richard, 63
PDSs movement. *See* Professional development schools movement
Peck, R.F., & Tucker, J.A., 26, 28
peer coaching programs, 13, 23
peer collaboration, 41
peer observation, 53
perceptions in approach to innovation, 66
performance-based certification, 26
Perkins, D.J., 5, 44. *See also* Tishman, S.
permissiveness in constructivism, 45–46
personality
    affected by classroom isolation, 19
    in collaboration, viii–ix, 3
personalization (conversation prompt), 106. *See also* Ownership
perspectives, multiple, 61–62
Peterson, P.L. *See* Elmore, R.F.
Piaget, Jean
    contributions to constructivism, 45
    education, 39
Picasso, Pablo, 4
Pintrich, R.R., ix
planning, 15, *54*
planning time, use of, 86. *See also* Preparation time
plateauing (conversation prompt), 109
policymakers, *92*

and educational research, 88
    as users of *Framework,* 83
    value of collaboration, 86
political power plays and staff development, 52
political trends, 33
Posner, B.Z. *See* Kouzes, J.M.
Postman, N., 32
postmodernism, 37
Pounder, D.G., 11
Power, B.M. *See* Hubbard, R.S.
power relationships, 56, *77*. *See also* Relationships
powerfulness, perceptions of, 22
practitioner inquiry. *See* Teacher/practitioner research
practitioner research. *See* Teacher/practitioner research
prepackaged teachers' materials, 39
preparation and professionalism (conversation prompt), 97, 119
preparation time. *See also* Planning time, use of
    common, 71
    contrived collegiality in, 13
preparedness (conversation prompt), 117
preschool (conversation prompt), 122
principals. *See also* Administrators
    collaboration with teachers, 9
    empowering teachers, 92
    fostering collaboration, 12
    role of, 15
problem-solving
    and collaboration, 11
    models of, 9–10
    and social learning, 40
    and teacher as learner, 79
    vs. creative thinking, 64
professional development
    collaborative view of, 52–53
    conversation prompt, 105
    isolation as barrier to, 23
    in Japan, 89
    local programs, 55
    need for system of, 26
    in professional community, 47–48

and professional fulfillment, 23
and school achievement, 53, 56
and teacher research, 49, 50
"trainer of trainer" institutes, 47
professional development schools movement
and collaboration, 10
and local district, 54–56
and teacher education reform, 27
professional fulfillment and satisfaction, 23, 25, 82
professional identity, 76, 81
professional orientation of new teachers, 6
professionalism
in approach to innovation, 66
conversation prompt, 97
psychic rewards, 23. *See also* Professional fulfillment and satisfaction
public education, societal influences on, 32–36
public policy issues and teacher education, 27
Pugach, M.C., & Johnson, L.J. *See also* Johnson, L.J.
collaborative learning environment, 11
site-based management, 9

R
Ray, K. *See* Winer, M.
reading specialists. *See also* Resource educators
perspectives on collaboration, 92
standards, 30, 72, 87
reflective practice
as benefit, 83
and collaborative experience, 28
conversation prompt, 120
in groups, 43, 90
and job-embedded learning, 53
process of, 16
and professional identity, 76
in teacher education reform, 29
in teacher research, 49, 50

Rehabilitation Act of 1973, 35
relationships, *21. See also* Collaborative relationships; Power relationships
conversation prompt, 111
interpersonal, 20
relationships, caring, 49
resource educators
conversation prompt, 120
standards for, 30–32
respect
conversation prompt, 96
in *Framework*, 74
teaching lacking in, 22
respect for the student
conversation prompt, 101, 110, 112, 114, 118
mindful perspective, 61–62
results-driven education, 53
Richardson, V., 55–56
Riley, Richard, 31–32, 37
risk-taking, *23*, 119 (conversation prompt)
Rogers, Richard, 4
Rogoff, B., 41
Rogoff, B., & Lave, J., 41
Rosenholtz, S.J.
criticisms of collaboration, 11–12
teacher productivity, 23
Rubin, H., 16
Russell, T. *See* Munby, H.

S
Sarason, Seymour B.
definition of collaboration, 3
interesting experiences, 21
teachers' habits and belief systems, viii
SBM (site-based management), 9–10
Schmuck, R.A. *See* Taylor, V.S.
Schön, D.A.
creativity, 6, 8
nature of practical knowledge, 29
reflective practice, 28
school achievement and professional development, 53
school buddy system, 85–94
school district protocols, *53*
school districts
control of professional development, 56

and university teacher education programs, 54
school learning community, xi, 52
school librarians. *See also* Resource educators
creativity of, 7
roles of, xi
standards, 30–31, 72, 87
school library (conversation prompt), 98, 104
school psychologists and collaboration, 92
school reform
at classroom level, 24–25
movements toward, 87–88
school social workers, 92
Schrage, Michael, 3
science, collaboration in, 4
Scott, J.J. *See* Smith, S.C.
Section 504 (Rehabilitation Act of 1973), 35
self-awareness
and habits of mind, 67
and metacognition, 58
self-confidence in teachers, 22
self-knowledge
as result of collaboration, 2
and sharing knowledge, 7–8
self-reliance by teachers, 12
Senge, P.M., 52
Senge, P.M. et al., 3
sensitivity (conversation prompt), 104
shared language. *See* Common or shared language
shop talk
benefit of, 19
in teacher research, 49
Sinaiko, H. L., 2
site-based management (SBM), 9–10
Sizer, Theodore R.
critical friends groups, 64
school reform, 87
teacher characteristics, 22
Slavin, R.E., 41–42
Smith, S.C., & Scott, J.J., 9
social development, 45
social interactions working against collaboration, 12–13
social justice
and collaborative partnerships, 68–70
teacher education for, 6

social learners, 44
social learning
    collaboration in, 11
    teaching of, 40–43
socialization of teachers, 24. *See also* Culture of teaching
Socrates, 1–2
Solomon, M.Z. *See* Morocco, C.C.
sounding boards, *48*
Sparks, D., & Hirsh, S., 53
special education, *87*
    contrived collegiality with, 13
    legal requirements for, 35
    and team management, 10
special education resource educators, 31. *See also* Resource educators
special education teachers
    conversation prompt, 126
    perspectives on collaboration, 92
    standards, 72, 86–87
special needs children, 34–35
specialist teachers, 20. *See also* Resource educators
Sroufe, G.E., 88
staff developers, 47
staff development. *See* Professional development
standards
    for collaboration, 30, 72, 85
    encouraging research, 47–48
    facilitating collaboration, 78, 81, 83
    oppression by, 6
    for resource educators, 30
    in teacher education reform, 29
start-up energy, 7
Steffe, L.P., & Gale, J., 5, 16
Steinberg, L., 36
Sternberg, R.J., 39
Stevenson, R. *See* Noffke, S.
Stigler, J.W., & Hiebert, J.
    implementation, 86
    Japanese practice, 88–89
    principle of collaboration, 90
strengths and weaknesses, *44*, 74
structure
    affecting collaboration, 78, 82
    as highlight of *Framework*, 83
    in joint efforts, 15

student ability level (conversation prompt), 112
student learning
    improved by collaboration, 86
    and school reform, 90
student teachers (conversation prompt), 123
students
    conversation prompt, 101, 103, 112, 114, 126
    engagement and disengagement, 36, 44
    ownership by, 42
success
    conversation prompt, 98
    in creative thinking, 66
    recognition of, 63
Sullivan, Arthur, 4
support staff as part of learning community, xi
synergy and collaborative process
    conversation prompt, 124
    ingredients for, 79
systems thinking, 53

T
Tafel, L.S., & Fischer, J.C., 49
Taylor, V.S., Thompson, K., & Schmuck, R.A., 52
teachable moments (conversation prompt), 126
teacher-centered instruction
    disadvantages of, 44
    persistence of, 24
    transition to learner-centered instruction, 27–28, 55
teacher development. *See* Professional development
teacher education
    in constructivism, 5
    need for, 2–3
    policies for, 88
    problems with, 26
    in professional orientation of new teachers, 6
    undergraduate, 28
    vs. medical education, 20, 54
teacher education research and policy makers, 31
teacher educators as users of *Framework*, 83

teacher inquiry. *See also* Teacher/practitioner research
    local control of, 55–56
    in teacher research, 50
teacher inquiry groups
    in Japan, 89–90
    job-embedded learning, 53
    licensing, 29
    loss of meaning, 23
teacher/practitioner research. *See also* Teacher inquiry
    and academic community, 47
    obstacles to, 48–49
teacher-researcher collaboration, 14
teacher talk, 44
teachers
    burnt-out, 83
    dreams, 25
    ideal characteristics of, 87
    as users of *Framework*, 83
teachers, beginning
    conversation prompt, 109
    isolation of, 20
teachers as learners
    and cooperative learning, 90
    need for, 25
    ownership, 49, 56
    recruitment, 27
    salaries, 28
teaching strategies and teacher as learner, 79
team efforts in business, 15
team management, 9
teaming, 11
technical work and inquiry, 55
technology
    and collaborative process, 7
    effect of change, 34
    trends in, 32
textbooks, 44
theory base, *51*
"theory" course work *vs.* practice, 29
thinking
    in constructivism, 44
    teaching of, 38–40
thinking and leadership (conversation prompt), 96
thinking processes
    as dimension of thinking, 39
    and metacognition, 58
thinking styles, 62

Third International Mathematics and Science Study (TIMSS), 88–89
Thompson, K. *See* Taylor, V.S.
Thornton, L.J., & McEntee, M.E., 57
threats to professional standing, 12
time, *28, 49, 83*
    affecting collaboration, 78, 82
    conversation prompt, 102, 111
time, taking, as habit of mind, 39
time frame in joint efforts, 15
TIMSS (Third International Mathematics and Science Study), 88–89
Tishman, S., Perkins, D.J., & Jay, E., 39
Toffler, A., 4
Toma, C. *See* Wertsch, J.V.
Tompkins, Jane
    constructivism, 5
    love of subjects, 25
transitions to shifts in perspectives, 54–55
trust (conversation prompt), 96
trusting environment
    in constructivism, 45
    in *Framework,* 72
Tucker, J.A. *See* Peck, R.F.
Tudge, J., 41
turnover, 20

U
underachieving students, 36
understanding in constructivism, 44

V
validity of teacher research, 51
values and beliefs
    in approach to innovation, 66
    and political trends, 33
    in teacher research, 49
veteran teachers *vs.* newbies (conversation prompt), 109
visualization in creative thinking, 65
Vygotsky, Lev
    contributions to constructivism, 45
    definition of collaboration, 3
    developmental processes, 40–41
    metacognitive mediation, 42

W
Wald, P.J., & Castleberry, M.S., 91–92
Waller, W.
    culture of teaching, 19
    shop talk, 49
    social nature of school, 25–26

Watson, James, 4
"we not I" philosophy, *89*
    conversation prompt, 103
    in leadership, 15
weakness. *See also* Failures, discussion of
    collaboration as, 20
    fear of revealing, 22
weaknesses and strengths, *44, 74*
Weber, Robert J., 11
Welch, M., 10
Wertsch, J.V., & Toma, C., 41
Whitehead, A.N., 1
Whiting, Charles S., 65
whole school concerns and classroom-only concerns, 55
Winer, M., & Ray, K., 15
Winitzky et al., 35
Wise, A.E., 29–30. *See also* Darling-Hammond, L.
Wozniak, Stephen, 4
Wright, Wilbur, & Orville, 4

Z
Zeichner, K., 31
Zemelman, S., Daniels, H., & Hyde, A., 11
zone of proximal development, 42–43

Gail Bush is Director, School Library Media Program, and Associate Professor, Graduate School of Library and Information Science, Dominican University, in River Forest, Illinois. For ten years, she was curriculum librarian in suburban Chicago at Maine West High School Library Resource Center, honored with the 1996 National School Library Media Program of the Year Award. Bush was named North Suburban Library System School Librarian of the Year in 1998–99 for her leadership in collaboration between her school program and the local public library. Her administrative experience includes work in corporate and academic libraries. She holds a Ph.D. in educational psychology from Loyola University Chicago and an M.S. in library science and a B.A. in anthropology from University of Illinois at Urbana–Champaign. A frequent speaker, Bush publishes articles on numerous topics including modeling for lifelong reading, poetry, information literacy, youth activism, and creativity.